M000004340

Practice Book

Teacher Edition
Grade 3

Harcourt School Publishers

www.harcourtschool.com

ISBN 10: 0-15-349885-4
ISBN 13: 978-0-15-349885-5

7 8 9 10 073 17 16 15 14 13 12 11 10 09

Contents

TWISTS AND TURNS

BREAKING NEW GROUND

Contents

TWISTS AND TURNS

BREAKING NEW GROUND

Name _____

▲ Read the Spelling Words. Write each word where it belongs. **Order will vary.**

Spelling Words

1. this
2. went
3. jump
4. still
5. last
6. dust
7. tell
8. drop
9. shut
10. lamp
11. stop
12. felt
13. drink
14. clock
15. stand

Words with Short *a*

1. last
2. lamp
3. stand

Words with Short *e*

4. went
5. tell
6. felt

Words with Short *i*

7. this
8. still
9. drink

Words with Short *o*

10. drop
11. stop
12. clock

Words with Short *u*

13. jump
14. dust
15. shut

School-Home Connection
Ask your child to help you write a grocery list. Have him or her point out the words that have short vowel sounds and circle the short vowel in each word.

▲ Read the words in the box. Write each word in the correct column below. You will write some words in more than one column.

this	went	jump	still	last
dust	tell	drop	shut	lamp
stop	felt	drink	clock	stand

Words that have the letter *t*	Words that have the letter *l*	Words that have the letter *p*
tap	luck	pen
sits	milk	tips
lost	ball	top
1. this	1. still	1. jump
2. went	2. last	2. drop
3. still	3. tell	3. lamp
4. last	4. lamp	4. stop
5. dust	5. felt	
6. tell	6. clock	
7. shut		
8. stop		
9. felt		
10. stand		

School-Home Connection

Write the following words on a sheet of paper: *past, dust, doll,* and *pull*. Ask the student which words end in -st. Then ask which words end in -ll.

▲ Read the story. Then circle the letter of the best answer to each question.

Maribel and Tracy played in Maribel's grassy backyard nearly every day. Maribel liked to take off her shoes and run barefoot. Tracy always warned her about that. "Watch out," she would say. "You might step on a sharp rock or a piece of glass."

"Don't worry," Maribel would answer. "I will be fine." One day after playing, Maribel put her shoes back on. "Yeow!" she screamed. Maribel's mom came running to help. Quickly, she removed a stinger from Maribel's heel. "There was a bee in your shoe," she told Maribel. Maribel stopped crying for a minute. "See," she said to Tracy. "Running barefoot was safe. It was my shoe that was dangerous!"

Tip What words help you tell when and where the action begins?

1. What is the setting of the story?
   A the lunch room
   B Maribel's house
   C the library
   (D) Maribel's yard

Tip Remember that the main character is usually the person who has a problem.

2. Who is the main character of the story?
   (A) Maribel
   B a teacher
   C a bee
   D a pair of shoes

Tip Remember that another character is someone who interacts with the main character.

3. Who is another character in the story?
   A a dog walker
   (B) Tracy
   C Ms. Hamilton
   D Maribel

School-Home Connection

Have the student select two or three words from the story. Then help him or her to understand what they mean. Together, write a sentence using each word.

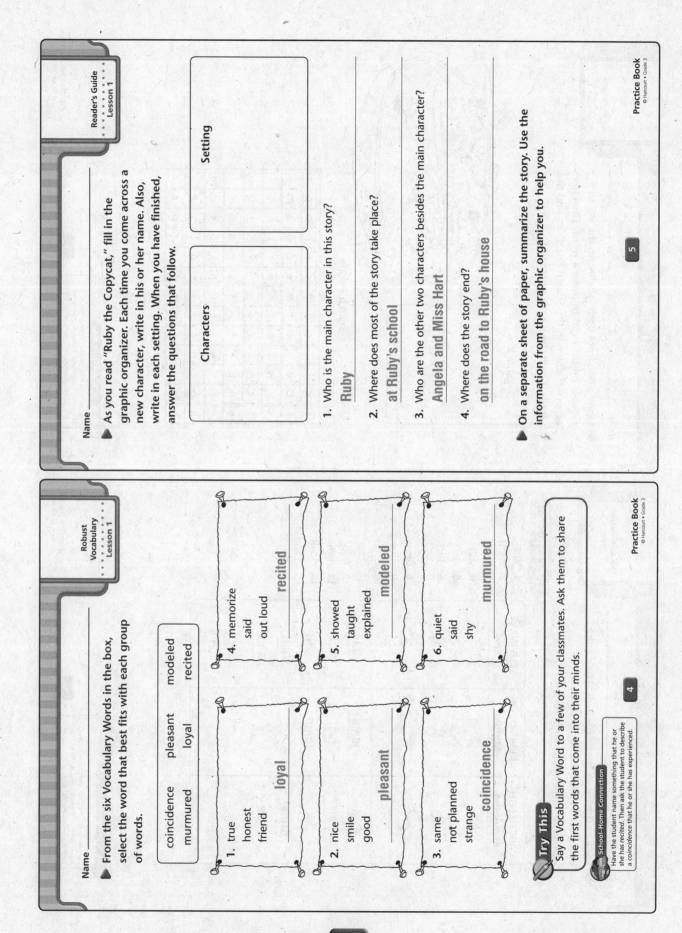

Robust Vocabulary — Lesson 1

Name _____

▲ From the six Vocabulary Words in the box, select the word that best fits with each group of words.

| coincidence | pleasant | modeled |
| murmured | loyal | recited |

1. true
   honest
   friend
   loyal

2. nice
   smile
   good
   pleasant

3. same
   not planned
   strange
   coincidence

4. memorize
   said
   out loud
   recited

5. showed
   taught
   explained
   modeled

6. quiet
   said
   shy
   murmured

Try This

Say a Vocabulary Word to a few of your classmates. Ask them to share the first words that come into their minds.

School-Home Connection

Have the student name something that he or she has *recited*. Then ask the student to describe a *coincidence* that he or she has experienced.

Reader's Guide — Lesson 1

Name _____

▲ As you read "Ruby the Copycat," fill in the graphic organizer. Each time you come across a new character, write in his or her name. Also, write in each setting. When you have finished, answer the questions that follow.

Characters

Setting

1. Who is the main character in this story?
   Ruby

2. Where does most of the story take place?
   at Ruby's school

3. Who are the other two characters besides the main character?
   Angela and Miss Hart

4. Where does the story end?
   on the road to Ruby's house

▲ On a separate sheet of paper, summarize the story. Use the information from the graphic organizer to help you.

Name _____

▲ Draw a line from each syllable on the left to a syllable on the right to make a word. Then look across or down in the Search Puzzle to find the words. Circle the words you made.

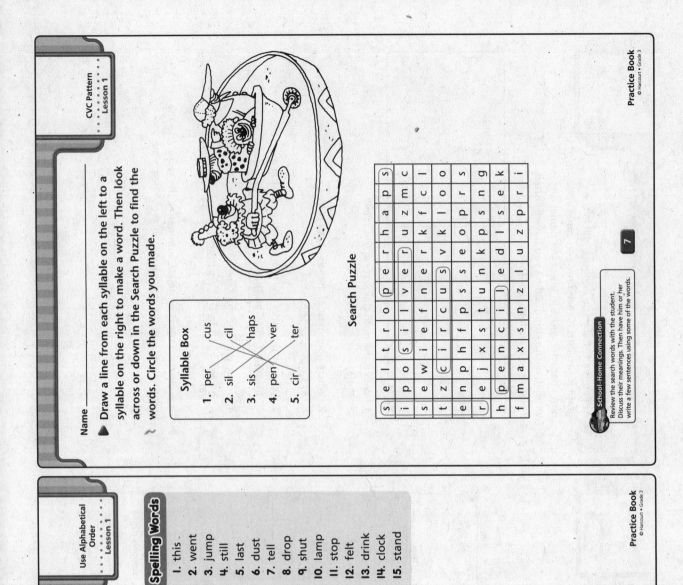

Syllable Box

1. per — cus
2. sil — cil
3. sis — haps
4. pen — ver
5. cir — ter

Search Puzzle

s	e	l	t	r	o	p	e	r	h	a	p	s
i	p	o	s	i	l	v	e	r	u	z	m	c
s	e	w	i	e	f	n	e	r	k	f	c	l
t	z	c	i	r	c	u	s	v	k	l	o	o
e	n	p	h	f	p	s	s	e	o	p	r	s
r	e	j	x	s	t	u	n	k	p	s	n	g
h	p	e	n	c	i	l	e	d	l	s	e	k
f	m	a	x	s	n	z	l	u	z	p	r	i

7

Practice Book
© Harcourt • Grade 3

School-Home Connection
Review the search words with the student. Discuss their meanings. Then have him or her write a few sentences using some of the words.

Name _____

▲ Look at the list of spelling words. Then write each word under the correct part of the alphabet—*beginning, middle,* or *end.*

Spelling Words

1. this
2. went
3. jump
4. still
5. last
6. dust
7. tell
8. drop
9. shut
10. lamp
11. stop
12. felt
13. drink
14. clock
15. stand

ABCDEFGH Beginning	IJKLMNOPQR Middle	STUVWXYZ End
dust	jump	this
drop	last	went
felt	lamp	still
drink		tell
clock		shut
		stop
		stand

6

Practice Book
© Harcourt • Grade 3

School-Home Connection
Have the student write down five of his or her favorite foods. Then ask whether each word would come at the beginning, in the middle, or at the end of the alphabet.

© Harcourt • Grade 3

Student Edition pp. 6–7

Statements and Questions — Lesson 1

Name _____

▲ Add the correct end mark to each sentence. Then label each as a *statement* or a *question*.

1. Where is the teacher **?** _____ question
2. I do not like to jump **.** _____ statement
3. When does Anita run **?** _____ question
4. Do you know Mr. Wang **?** _____ question
5. We play in the grass **.** _____ statement

▲ Rewrite each group of words to form a statement or a question. Put the words in an order that makes sense. Use capital letters and end marks correctly.

6. to the park I go (statement)
   I go to the park.

7. do walk you to school (question)
   Do you walk to school?

8. Willow ball the throws (statement)
   Willow throws the ball.

9. can Kurt play softball (statement)
   Kurt can play softball.

10. you can football play (question)
    Can you play football?

School-Home Connection
Work with your child to write two questions about your family and two statements that answer the questions.

Practice Book
© Harcourt • Grade 3

8

Base Words + Endings -ed, -ing — Lesson 2

Name _____

▲ Read the Spelling Words. Write each word where it belongs. Order will vary.

Words with -ed
1. saved
2. moved
3. pulled
4. hopped
5. picked
6. folded
7. shopped

Words with -ing
8. riding
9. waking
10. taking
11. baking
12. having
13. letting
14. running
15. drawing

School-Home Connection
Help your child make a list of words that have -ed and -ing endings. Discuss the correct spelling for each word. Confirm each word's spelling with your child, using a dictionary.

Practice Book
© Harcourt • Grade 3

9

Spelling Words
1. saved
2. moved
3. riding
4. waking
5. pulled
6. taking
7. hopped
8. baking
9. picked
10. having
11. letting
12. running
13. drawing
14. folded
15. shopped

7

Student Edition pp. 8–9

▲ Read the story. Circle the letter of the best answer to each question.

Marissa wanted to surprise her mother. She was going to paint a picture on a piece of wood. "What color should I use?" she thought.

In a closet, she found pails and pails of paint. There was blue, yellow, red, and every other color she could think of. "I will use every color!" she said to herself. Marissa started to paint. The wet colors mixed together.

Her painting was a mess. What could she do?

Just then, her mother came home. Crying, Marissa said, "I wanted to give you a special gift."

Her mother said, "Marissa, your gift *is* special to me. That is because you made it. It looks like a new kind of rainbow! Thank you for your hard work."

Marissa smiled. She helped her mother put the piece of wood on the wall, where they could see it every day.

Tip
Who is the most important person in the story?

1. Who is the story mostly about?
   A Marissa's mother
   B pails of paint
   C a rainbow
   Ⓓ Marissa

Tip
The main character's words and actions tell you how he or she feels.

2. How does the main character feel at the end of the story?
   Ⓐ happy
   B angry
   C sad
   D mixed-up

Tip
Where do most things happen in the story?

3. What is the setting of the story?
   A a paint store
   Ⓑ Marissa's house
   C a friend's house
   D Marissa's school

School-Home Connection
Ask the student to think about how he or she would improve the story. Brainstorm ideas about other possible characters and settings.

10   Practice Book
© Harcourt • Grade 3

▲ Read the story, and look at the two columns. In the correct column, write the root word for each underlined verb.

Yesterday afternoon, my mom was driving us home from a family cookout. I stared out the window. "Mom!" I yelled. "There's a gray cat on the road!" My mother braked hard and turned our car to the right. She stopped.

We got out of the car, and the cat walked right up to us. He closed his eyes and purred. I could tell that he liked me a lot. But just then his owner came for him. I told her that I hoped I could have a cat of my own someday.

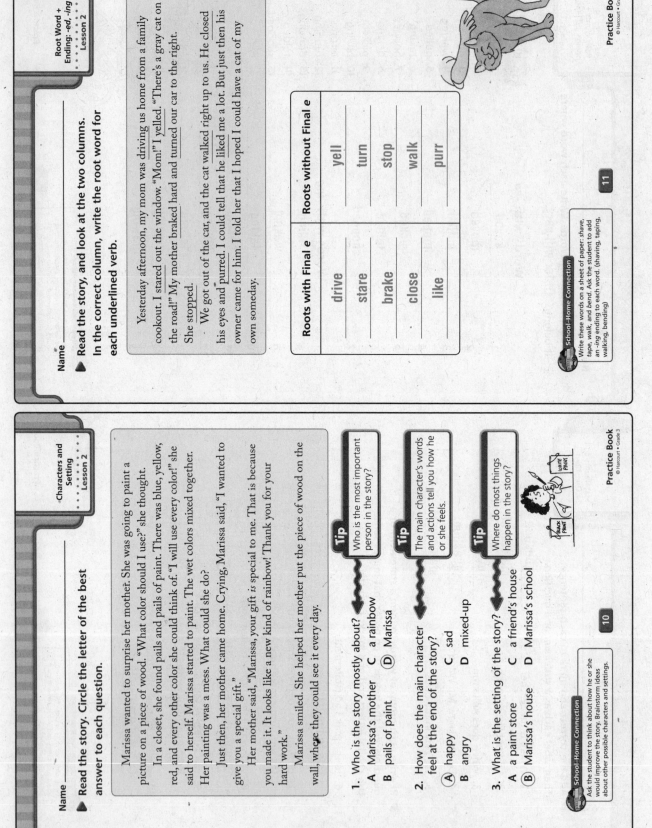

Roots with Final e	Roots without Final e
drive	yell
stare	turn
brake	stop
close	walk
like	purr

School-Home Connection
Write these words on a sheet of paper: *shave, tape, walk,* and *bend.* Ask the student to add an *-ing* ending to each word. (shaving, taping, walking, bending)

11   Practice Book
© Harcourt • Grade 3

Name _____

▲ Read each question and the underlined
Vocabulary Word. Write a sentence to answer
each question. **Possible responses are shown.**

1. If you were going to an assembly, would you expect to see one
person or many people?
I would expect to see many people.

2. My little brother squirmed at the doctor's office. Did he sit quietly or
did he move around a lot?
He moved around a lot.

3. If a singer autographed a CD for you, did she sing her name or sign
her name?
She signed her name.

4. Mr. Jones will dismiss the class at three o'clock. Do you think a lot of
people or no people will be left at three-thirty?
No people will be left.

5. When I make a picture that is a patchwork of color, should I use one
color or many colors?
You should use many colors.

6. If you brought plenty of food to a picnic, would there be not
enough food or more than enough food?
There would be more than enough food.

Try This

Say a Vocabulary Word to a partner. Ask your partner to use it in
a sentence.

School-Home Connection
Have the student act out *squirmed* and
autographed. Ask the student to show how his
or her teacher dismisses the class.

12

Name _____

▲ Fill in the characters, setting, and story events
as you read "The Day Eddie Met the Author."
Possible responses are shown.

Section 1 pages 58–59

Characters: Eddie,
Mrs. Morrow, author

Setting:
school

First: Everyone seems excited about
meeting the author.

Next:
Eddie writes a question.

Section 2 pages 60–65

Then:
Eddie and others wait to ask their questions.

Section 3 pages 66–74

Last:
The author answers Eddie's question.

▲ Use the information in this chart to write a summary of "The Day Eddie
Met the Author." Write your summary on another sheet of paper.

13

Name _____

▲ Read each root word in the left column. Circle the correct spelling of the word when the ending -ed or -ing is added.

1. save   (saved)   saveed
2. hop   hoped   (hopped)
3. ride   rideing   (riding)
4. take   (taking)   takeing
5. dine   dineed   (dined)
6. let   leting   (letting)
7. shop   shoped   (shopped)
8. run   runing   (running)
9. tip   (tipping)   tiping
10. wake   (waked)   wakeed
11. jump   jumpped   (jumped)
12. step   (stepped)   steped
13. tell   teling   (telling)
14. lift   liftting   (lifting)
15. skip   (skipping)   skiping

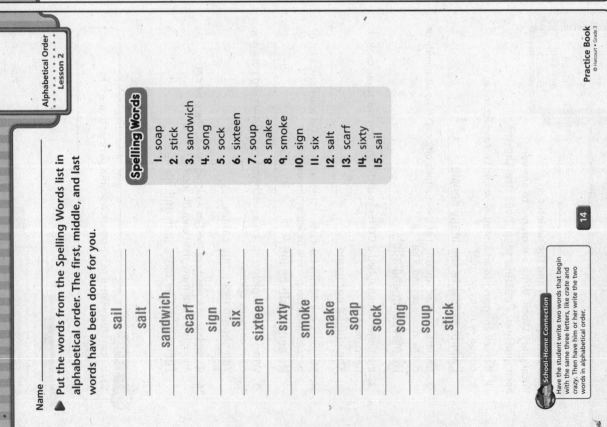

School-Home Connection
Have the student read aloud the words from the list above. Then help him or her write short sentences for five of the words.

15

Practice Book
© Harcourt • Grade 3

Name _____

▲ Put the words from the Spelling Words list in alphabetical order. The first, middle, and last words have been done for you.

Spelling Words
1. soap
2. stick
3. sandwich
4. song
5. sock
6. sixteen
7. soup
8. snake
9. smoke
10. sign
11. six
12. salt
13. scarf
14. sixty
15. sail

sail
salt
sandwich
scarf
sign
six
sixteen
sixty
smoke
snake
soap
sock
song
soup
stick

School-Home Connection
Have the student write two words that begin with the same three letters, like crate and crazy. Then have him or her write the two words in alphabetical order.

14

Practice Book
© Harcourt • Grade 3

© Harcourt • Grade 3

Student Edition pp. 14–15

© Harcourt • Grade 3

Name ____________

Commands and Exclamations
Lesson 2

▶ If the sentence is complete, add a correct end mark. If the sentence is not complete, write *not a sentence.* Possible responses are shown.

1. My father is an author .
2. How he loves to write !
3. How do I help him ?
4. Things that he can write about not a sentence
5. Read his latest book .
6. Wow, it's exciting !

▶ Add words and end marks to make four kinds of sentences. Each sentence is started for you. Possible responses are shown.

7. a statement
You have brown eyes.
8. a command
Go to school.
9. an exclamation
What a nice day it is!
10. a question
What are you doing?

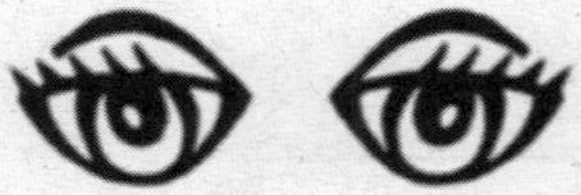

School-Home Connection
Work with your child to write a question and a command about the town where you live. The command should be related to the question.

Name ____________

Long Vowel Digraphs /ē/ee, ea; /ā/ai, ay; /ō/oa, ow
Lesson 3

▶ Read the Spelling Words. Write each word where it belongs. Order will vary.

Spelling Words
1. deep
2. play
3. lean
4. glow
5. team
6. away
7. slow
8. trail
9. dream
10. stain
11. toast
12. speed
13. raise
14. sweet
15. layer

Words with *ee*
1. deep
2. speed
3. sweet

Words with *ea*
4. lean
5. team
6. dream

Words with *ai*
7. trail
8. stain
9. raise

Words with *ay*
10. play
11. away
12. layer

Words with *oa* or *ow*
13. glow
14. slow
15. toast

School-Home Connection
Work with your child to list words that have long vowel sounds spelled: ee, ea, ai, ay, oa, or ow. Have your child circle the vowels that spell the long vowel sound.

Locate Information
Lesson 3

▲ Read the title page below. Then write the answers to the questions.

Animals That Bark and Meow
How to Take Care of Them

Brianna X. Fieldman
Chief Veterinarian at Oakland Animal Hospital

Deartown Publishers

1. What do you think this book is about?
Possible response: how to take care of dogs and cats

2. What does the information about the author tell about the book? Explain.
Possible response: The author is the Chief Veterinarian at an animal hospital, so she must know a lot about pets like dogs and cats.

3. What is the name of the publisher?
Deartown Publishers

18

Vowel digraphs:
*ee, ea; ai, ay;
oa, ow*
Lesson 3

▲ Read the long /ē/, /ā/ and /ō/ words in the box below. Then complete the paragraph. Write each word where it makes the most sense.

deep	lean	speed	team	laid	know	row
reach	dream	least	sleep	playing	boat	

Last night, I __laid__ awake for a while in bed, then I went to __sleep__ just after 9:00. I had a very strange __dream__. I was __playing__ with some people from my basketball __team__. We were standing on a hill that was at __least__ a mile high! When I looked down, it was like looking into a __deep__ hole. I didn't __know__ why we were there. Then I began to __lean__ back against a fence, but I broke right through it! I grabbed for one of my friends, but I couldn't quite __reach__ her. Then I began to fall. At first I fell slowly, but I soon began to __speed__ toward the ground. Just before I hit the bottom, I landed in a __boat__ and began to __row__ it up the river. When I woke up, I found I was in my bed, not on a river, and it was morning already!

19

Name _____

▲ Answer each question about one of the Vocabulary Words.

1. If I want a certain book, do I care about which book I get?

   Possible response: Yes, because a different book might

   not interest me or be the one I want.

2. If you were going to tell me about your family's culture, what is something you could talk about?

   Possible response: the type of food my family eats, or

   where my family is from

3. When you work with a tutor, how will he or she help you?

   Possible response: He or she will help me study or learn

   something.

4. What is an example of chores you do at home?

   Possible response: I make my bed and sweep the kitchen.

5. What kind of workers wear uniforms?

   Possible response: police officers, doctors

6. What are some resources you would need to grow flowers?

   Possible response: seeds, dirt, water, sunlight

Try This

Choose a Vocabulary Word and make up a sentence using the word. Then say the sentence without the Vocabulary Word, and have a partner repeat the sentence with the correct word filled in.

School-Home Connection

Ask the student to write three sentences using the Vocabulary Words on this page.

20

Name _____

▲ Use the chart to help you organize and locate information from the story "Schools Around the World." Write the title in the first box. Write headings in the boxes just below the title. Write the main ideas in the boxes under each heading.

Title
Schools Around the World

Heading School Buildings	**Heading** **Getting to School**	**Heading** **School Clothing**
The main idea is that the kind of school buildings children have depend on where they live.	**Children travel to school in many ways, depending on how far they have to go.**	**The kind of clothing children wear depends on the climate.**

▲ Use information from the chart above to write a summary of the selection on a separate sheet of paper.

21

13

▲ Read the words in each Word Box. Write the words in alphabetical order between the guide words.

leap	lean	layer	less	lady

lady

1. lady
2. layer
3. lean
4. leap
5. less

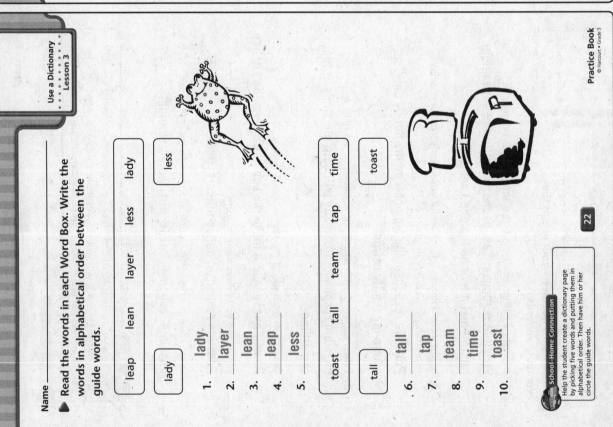

toast	tall	team	tap	time

tall

6. tall
7. tap
8. team
9. time
10. toast

toast

Practice Book
© Harcourt • Grade 3

▲ Read the first word in dark print in each row. Circle another word in the row that has the same vowel sound.

1. speed   hen   (treat)   play

2. shape   (drain)   slow   sheep

3. grow   flop   (broke)   grain

4. tray   (wade)   wide   with

5. beast   (tree)   best   bay

6. poke   step   steep   (roast)

7. mail   man   mill   (may)

8. oats   eats   (bowl)   aims

9. gray   spike   cart   (face)

10. Pete   (steam)   rate   check

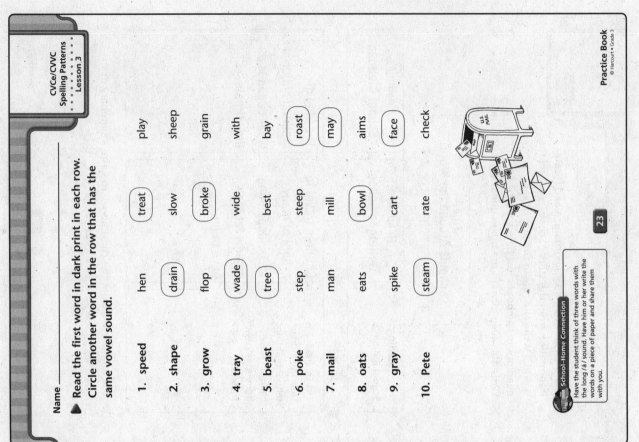

Practice Book
© Harcourt • Grade 3

Complete and Simple Subjects and Predicates
Lesson 3

Name _____

▲ Add a complete subject to each predicate.
Then underline the simple subject. **Possible responses are shown.**

1. The good student _____ went to school.
2. Three boys _____ played outside.
3. The hungry children _____ ate lunch.
4. The little girl _____ took a nap.
5. Some dancers _____ performed on stage.
6. The new house _____ was made of brick.

▲ Add a complete predicate to each subject. Then underline the simple predicate. **Possible responses are shown.**

7. An art teacher came to our classroom _____
8. The excited children jumped up and down _____
9. He walked to the store _____
10. My mother helped me study _____
11. The school was on the corner _____
12. The tired baby closed her eyes _____

School-Home Connection
Work with your child to write two sentences about your city or town. Ask your child to circle the simple subject and underline the simple predicate in each sentence.

24

Practice Book
© Harcourt • Grade 3

Plurals s, es
Lesson 4

Spelling Words

1. ants
2. toys
3. flies
4. things
5. boxes
6. games
7. lines
8. rocks
9. wishes
10. ladies
11. dishes
12. babies
13. bushes
14. glasses
15. puppies

Name _____

▲ Read the Spelling Words. Write each word where it belongs. **Order may vary.**

Base Word with -s

1. ants
2. toys
3. things
4. games
5. lines
6. rocks

Base Word with -es

7. flies
8. boxes
9. wishes
10. ladies
11. dishes
12. babies
13. bushes
14. glasses
15. puppies

School-Home Connection
With your child, walk outside and look for groups of plants or objects. Help your child list objects you see, such as bushes, bikes, and houses. Discuss the correct spelling for each word.

25

Practice Book
© Harcourt • Grade 3

Name _____

▲ Complete each sentence with the plural form of a word from the box. Be sure to use the correct ending, -s or -es.

beach	book	box	dime	tree
dress	flash	inch	side	river

1. Shelby tried on three __dresses__ before she found the one she liked best.

2. Florida has some of the most famous sandy __beaches__ in the world.

3. I like to read __books__ about outer space.

4. A triangle has three __sides__.

5. Ms. Green bought two __boxes__ of cereal at the grocery store.

6. I saw some __flashes__ of lightning in the sky last night.

7. A foot is 12 __inches__ long.

8. One dollar amounts to the same as ten __dimes__.

9. The maple __trees__ have colorful leaves in the autumn.

10. People can fish in the many __rivers__ that run through the northwest.

School–Home Connection
Ask the student to spell the plural forms of the words in the box without looking at the paper.

27

Practice Book
© Harcourt • Grade 3

Name _____

▲ Use the Table of Contents to answer the questions. Write your answers in order on the lines.

The History of Outer Space
Table of Contents

1. What is the title of the fourth chapter?
   "Space in the Middle Ages"

2. What is the title of the chapter that begins on page 3?
   "Why Study Space?"

3. On what page would you begin reading "Space in Ancient History"?
   page 15

4. What is the first page of the Index?
   page 60

5. What is the title of the second chapter?
   "Who Studies Space?"

School–Home Connection
With the student, brainstorm possible ideas that might be covered in Chapter 1: "Why Study Space?"

26

Practice Book
© Harcourt • Grade 3

© Harcourt • Grade 3

Name _____

▲ Write the Vocabulary Word from the box that goes with each meaning.

apply	disappointed	invention

1. __disappointed__ unhappy about the way things worked out

2. __apply__ to fill out papers to do something, such as get a job

3. __invention__ something new that someone makes or creates

▲ Answer these questions about the Vocabulary Words from the box.

talented	research	hinder

4. What are some things that a talented person might be able to do?
__Possible response: play many musical instruments__

5. What is something you might do research about?
__Possible response: different kinds of dogs__

6. If you hinder someone, are you helping her or not helping her?
__You are not helping someone if you hinder her.__

School-Home Connection

With the student, discuss the meanings of any Vocabulary Words that he or she does not understand. Then have the student create a definition for each word.

28

Name _____

▲ As you read "Ellen Ochoa: Astronaut," pay attention to the order in which events are told. Fill in the graphic organizer as you read.

Childhood	She was born in Los Angeles, California. Her mother worked very hard. Ellen never dreamed of being an astronaut.
School Years	Ellen was a top student. She worked hard in school. Ellen loved music and math.
Adulthood	Ellen became a musician, an inventor, a pilot, and an astronaut. In 1993, she flew on the space shuttle, Discovery.

29

Name _____

▲ Write the plural form of each noun. Then circle the plural words in the Word Search.

1. country — countries
2. cage — cages
3. story — stories
4. lunch — lunches
5. tree — trees
6. fork — forks
7. tray — trays
8. party — parties
9. set — sets
10. book — books

Word Search

```
B D T R N W A F O R K E S L H
W C A Y Z E C O U N T R I E S
T R E E S L M R W Q I P Z B T
R G S A A C I K U P F C C O O
A S D D P Q A S L E O A H O R
Y E Y P A R T I E S D G U K I
S T O R Y S T E D A E E A S E
E S L U N C H E S S M I S
```

School–Home Connection
Ask the student to find the plural form of the word fox in the Word Search.

Practice Book
© Harcourt • Grade 3

31

Name _____

▲ Review the sample dictionary page and answer the questions. Write your answers on the lines.

dozen   dream

dozen (duhz•uhn) noun a group of 12

drag (drag) verb 1 to haul 2 to trail along the surface 3 to hang behind

drama (dra•muh) noun 1 a play for theater or television 2 an exciting or dangerous situation

draw (draw) verb 1 to use a pen or pencil to create a picture 2 to pull or move to the side 3 to inhale

dread (dred) noun a fear of something bad that might happen

dream (dreem) verb 1 to think and see images while you sleep 2 to imagine a possibility

1. What part of speech is the word dozen? noun

2. How many definitions does this dictionary give for the word draw? three

3. Read the sentence: The box was so heavy that I had to drag it across the floor. Which definition number of drag is used in this sentence? definition 2

4. What word means "a group of 12"? dozen

5. Write a sentence using the word dream. Possible response: I like to dream about going to outer space.

School–Home Connection
Have the student pronounce all six words and use each one in a sentence.

Practice Book
© Harcourt • Grade 3

30

Name _____

Compound Subjects and Predicates
Lesson 4

▲ Add a compound subject or a compound predicate to complete each sentence. Possible responses are shown.

1. Rita and Max _____ studied art.

2. The athletes ran and swam _____.

3. The music student practiced and performed _____.

4. Elena and her best friend _____ took dance classes.

5. The actor smiled and waved _____.

6. The boy and girl _____ watched the stars.

▲ Rewrite each sentence. Add commas where they belong. Draw one line under each compound subject and two lines under each compound predicate.

7. The soccer player ran kicked and scored.
The soccer player ran, kicked, and scored.

8. Exercise rest and healthful food made the swimmer strong.
Exercise, rest, and healthful food made the swimmer strong.

9. Raja his sister and his brother were good students.
Raja, his sister, and his brother were good students.

10. The scientist wrote a book won a prize and gave a speech.
The scientist wrote a book, won a prize, and gave a speech.

School-Home Connection
Work with your child to write one sentence about his or her day using a compound subject and one sentence using a compound predicate.

Name _____

Phonics Review: CVC and VCCV Patterns
Lesson 5

▲ Part A. Read the sentences. Find one CVC word and one VCCV word in each sentence. Write the words in the spaces below each sentence.

1. Rihanna's dog is such a rascal!

CVC: dog   VCCV: rascal

2. Hilary drew a beautiful picture on the wooden box.

CVC: box   VCCV: picture

3. The runner wore a baseball cap during the race.

CVC: cap   VCCV: runner

4. Just give the ball a tap with the racket.

CVC: tap   VCCV: racket

5. There is rubber cement in the den.

CVC: den   VCCV: rubber

▲ Part B. Choose one CVC word and one VCCV word from Part A, and write a short story using both words.
Accept reasonable responses.

_____

_____

_____

_____

School-Home Connection
Ask the student to find the short vowel sounds in racket and rubber.

Name _____

▲ Fold the paper along the dotted line. As each spelling word is read aloud, write it in the blank. Then unfold your paper and check your work. Practice writing any spelling words you missed.

Spelling Words

1. clock
2. drink
3. hopped
4. moved
5. waking
6. folded
7. stain
8. layer
9. team
10. slow
11. toast
12. ladies
13. flies
14. bushes
15. games

1. _____
2. _____
3. _____
4. _____
5. _____
6. _____
7. _____
8. _____
9. _____
10. _____
11. _____
12. _____
13. _____
14. _____
15. _____

Name _____

▲ Read the story. Write the root word for each underlined word in the correct column below the story.

Yesterday afternoon, I was feeling a little bored. I sat and <u>looked</u> out our front window, <u>waiting</u> for something to happen.

As I was <u>staring</u> down the street, a boy <u>skipped</u> by with the strangest dog I had ever seen. I went outside, <u>closing</u> the door behind me.

The boy <u>turned</u> and <u>faced</u> me. "This is Twinkletoes," he said. "We have a big show tomorrow."

I <u>glanced</u> again at his pet. "Is it a dog show?" I asked.

Just then, Twinkletoes oinked. "Oh, no," said the boy. "It is a show at the State Fair. Twinkletoes is a pig!"

As Twinkletoes and the boy <u>walked</u> down the street, I was sorry for <u>thinking</u> my street was boring!

Root Words with Final e

stare _____

close _____

face _____

glance _____

Root Words without Final e

feel _____

look _____

wait _____

walk _____

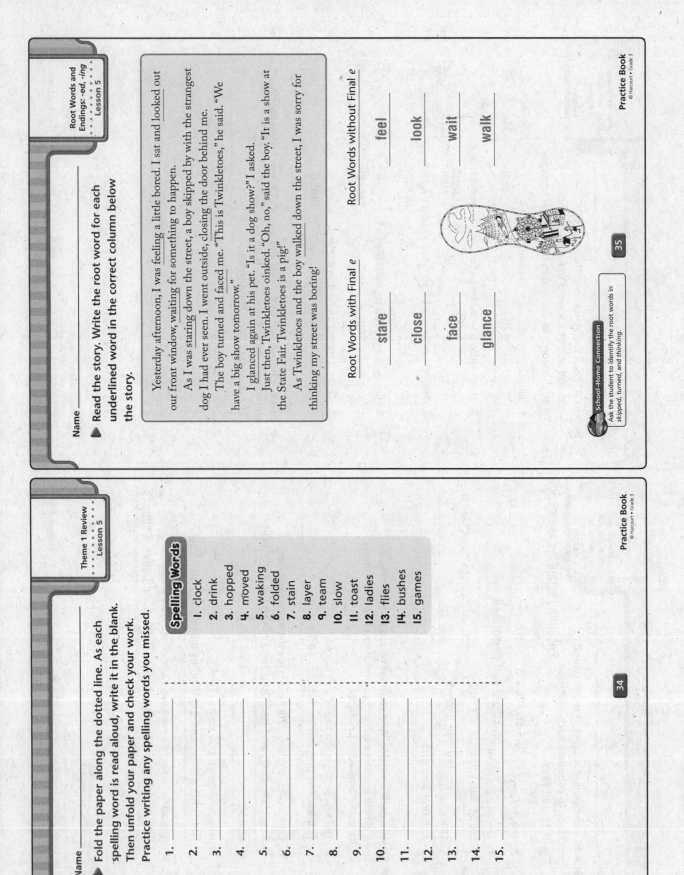

School-Home Connection
Ask the student to identify the root words in *skipped, turned,* and *thinking.*

Name _____

▲ Read the story. Circle the letter of the best answer to each question.

Lin's father was working very hard to open a new restaurant. He was nervous and very grouchy. One day, Lin decided to cheer him up. She sneaked into the restaurant with a handful of flowers she had picked. She said to herself, "These will look pretty on the tables. They will make Dad happy."

That night at bedtime, Lin's father came to say good night. "Sleep tight, Lin," he said. He turned off the lights and started to close the door. "Good night, Dad," she said. She was disappointed that he had not noticed the flowers. Then her father turned the lights back on. "I almost forgot," he said, pulling a flower from his shirt pocket and smiling. "I will make a big breakfast for us in the morning!"

1. Who are the characters in this story?
   A Lin and her mother
   B a father and son
   C Lin and her father

2. How can you tell that Lin's father is happy at the end of the story?
   A He smiles at Lin and says he will make her a big breakfast.
   B He says "Good night, Lin."
   C He is always sad.

3. Where does the story take place?
   A a movie theater
   B a restaurant and Lin's house
   C a friend's house

School–Home Connection
Have the student describe Lin and explain how he or she knows what Lin is like.

Name _____

▲ Read this part of a student's rough draft. Then answer the questions that follow.

(1) There is something new in Room 112 (2) Can you guess what it is (3) our rabbit has four babies. (4) How tiny the bunnies are! (5) Wish could take one home. (6) Do you bunnies like?

1. Which sentence should end with a period?
   A Sentence 1
   B Sentence 2
   C Sentence 4
   D Sentence 6

2. Which sentence should end with a question mark?
   A Sentence 1
   B Sentence 2
   C Sentence 3
   D Sentence 4

3. In which sentence are the words in an order that does not make sense?
   A Sentence 2
   B Sentence 3
   C Sentence 4
   D Sentence 6

4. Which word in Sentence 3 should be capitalized?
   A our
   B rabbit
   C four
   D babies

5. Which of the following is NOT a complete sentence?
   A Sentence 1
   B Sentence 3
   C Sentence 4
   D Sentence 5

6. Which sentence is correct as it is?
   A Sentence 3
   B Sentence 4
   C Sentence 5
   D Sentence 6

Name _____

▲ Underline the letters that make the long vowel sound in each word. Then circle the word whose vowel sound is different from the other two in the line.

1. bait   (freeze)   away

2. treat   feed   (goal)

3. (essay)   throw   goat

4. (crow)   drain   tray

5. mean   (complain)   see

6. snow   bowl   (beak)

7. reach   (delay)   feel

8. way   raise   (beep)

9. seal   (coast)   teeth

10. (heap)   know   oat

Name _____

▲ Complete the sentences below by putting the words in ( ) in alphabetical order and writing them in the blanks.

1. To compete in that race, you must be able to **bike** , **run** two miles, and **swim** 500 feet. (swim, bike, run)

2. Maxine puts her **doll** on her bed and leaves her **football** in the **garage** . (garage, football, doll)

3. For dinner last night, we had **chicken** with a side of **peas** and **potatoes** . (peas, potatoes, chicken)

4. Austin keeps his **bunny** in a **cage** , but his **cat** lives in the house. (bunny, cat, cage)

5. There were **leopards** and **lions** on the nature show, but there were no **lizards** . (lizards, leopards, lions)

6. You should travel by **plane** or **train** to get to Alaska from Florida. It is very far to travel there by **truck** . (truck, train, plane)

Name

Part A. Read the sentences below. Fill in the blanks with one of the Vocabulary Words from the Word Box.

| viewers | concealed | survive |
| independent | camouflage | donated |

1. When I taught myself how to tie my shoes, I felt __independent__.

2. Rico and Nate looked for bugs in their backyard. They checked under the log to see if any were __concealed__ there.

3. That television show is so funny! I am sure it has lots of __viewers__.

4. When Brenda outgrew her jacket, her mom __donated__ it to the thrift store.

5. A cactus can __survive__ without much water.

6. Claire used a pile of laundry as __camouflage__ when she hid in her messy bedroom.

Part B. Write one sentence that uses any two Vocabulary Words from above.

Possible response: Many animals survive in the wild by using camouflage.

School-Home Connection
Ask the student to think of three different animals that can survive in desert environments.

Name

Change the underlined noun to its plural form so that the sentence is correct. Write the new word on the line.

1. I found a basket of kitten on the sidewalk. __kittens__

2. Murat loves to collect butterfly. __butterflies__

3. There are four different juice mix in our pantry. __mixes__

4. Brodie has three wrench in his tool kit. __wrenches__

5. The workers built the shed with hammers and nail. __nails__

6. Martina blows kiss to her friends as she gets on the bus. __kisses__

7. Everyone in the class gave speech yesterday. __speeches__

8. Why do you think clowns have red nose? __noses__

9. It is good to give flower water and sunlight. __flowers__

10. Carol carry two suitcases when she travels overseas. __carries__

School-Home Connection
Ask the student to say the plural form of the nouns activity, princess, and group.

Grammar–Writing Connection
Lesson 5

▲ **Read this part of a student's rough draft. Then answer the questions that follow.**

(1) Eric watched the news on TV. (2) His father watched the news on TV. (3) The newscaster talked about special events. (4) A police officer a firefighter and a teacher taught third graders about safety. (5) The mayor took a trip and gave a speech.

1. Which is the simple subject of Sentence 1?
   Ⓐ Eric
   B Eric watched
   C the news
   D watched the news on TV

2. Which is the complete predicate of Sentence 3?
   A the newscaster
   B the newscaster talked
   C talked
   Ⓓ talked about special events

3. What is missing in Sentence 4?
   Ⓐ commas
   B a subject
   C a simple predicate
   D a complete predicate

4. Which sentence has a compound subject?
   A Sentence 1
   B Sentence 3
   Ⓒ Sentence 4
   D Sentence 5

5. Which sentence has a compound predicate?
   A Sentence 2
   B Sentence 3
   C Sentence 4
   Ⓓ Sentence 5

6. Which sentences could be joined to make one sentence with a compound subject?
   Ⓐ Sentences 1 and 2
   B Sentences 2 and 3
   C Sentences 3 and 4
   D Sentences 4 and 5

Review: Locate Information
Lesson 5

▲ **Use your *Student Edition* to answer the questions. Write the answers on the lines.**

1. Turn to page 22 and look at the illustration. What do you think is happening?
   Possible response: A shy student is starting school.

2. Turn to the table of contents. On which page does "The Singing Marvel" begin?
   page 42

3. Turn to page 89 and look at the photographs on the page. What do you think this page will be about?
   Possible response: School buildings in other countries.

4. Turn to page 106 and look at the illustrations. What do you think the story is about?
   The story could be about a family.

5. Turn to page 116 and look at the title. What do you think this selection is about?
   Possible response: I think it is about an astronaut.

6. What is the last page of the story, "Ellen Ochoa, Astronaut"?
   page 132

School–Home Connection
Ask the student to look at the picture on the cover of the *Student Edition* and write a possible caption for it.

Review: Use a Dictionary — Lesson 5

Name _____

▲ Review the sample dictionary page and answer the questions.

chase • cider

chase (chās) *verb* **1** to follow in order to catch someone or something. *noun* **2** the act of chasing.

cheap (chēp) *adjective* **1** low in cost, inexpensive. **2** of poor quality.

chick (chik) *noun* **1** a young chicken. *noun* **2** any young bird.

choose (chōōz) *verb* **1** to select. *verb* **2** to prefer (to do something).

cider (sī'dər) *noun* **1** juice pressed from fruits, usually apples.

1. What part of speech is the word *chick?* __noun__

2. How many definitions does this dictionary give for the word *choose?* __two__

3. Which definition of *cheap* is used in the following sentence?
These comic books are cheap, so I will buy three of them. __the first definition__

4. How many syllables does *cider* have? __two__

5. Which word can be a verb or a noun? __chase__

6. Which word has only one possible definition? __cider__

Compound Words — Lesson 6

Spelling Words

1. pickup
2. cannot
3. outside
4. bedroom
5. upstairs
6. raindrop
7. baseball
8. hallway
9. airplane
10. mailbox
11. sunshine
12. homework
13. classroom
14. something
15. playground

Name _____

▲ Make cards for the Spelling Words. Lay them down and read them.

1. Put the words with *up* in the first column.
2. Put the words with *room* in the second column.

The first one is done for you. **Order may vary.**

Words with *up*	Words with *room*
1. __pickup__	3. __bedroom__
2. __upstairs__	4. __classroom__

Words without *up* or *room*

5. __outside__
6. __mailbox__
7. __cannot__
8. __raindrop__
9. __baseball__
10. __hallway__
11. __airplane__
12. __sunshine__
13. __homework__
14. __something__
15. __playground__

▲ Read the passage. Then circle the letter of the best answer to each question.

The Sunshine Skyway Bridge in Florida was finished in 1987. Many people believe it is the most beautiful bridge in the world. It is painted yellow. I think the color is the reason that the bridge is so popular. Because of a terrible storm, 1,000 feet of that bridge fell into the bay. The Sunshine Skyway Bridge is 190 feet above the water at its highest point. It is held together by steel cables.

I feel that this bridge is the strongest bridge of all.

1. Which of the following sentences states a fact?
   (A) It is painted yellow.
   B I think the color is the reason that the bridge is so popular.
   C Many people believe it is the most beautiful bridge in the world.
   D I feel that this bridge is the strongest bridge of all.

2. Which of the following sentences is an opinion?
   A The Sunshine Skyway Bridge in Florida was finished in 1987.
   (B) I think the color is the reason that the bridge is so popular.
   C Another bridge once stood over Tampa Bay.
   D It is held together by steel cables.

3. Read the underlined sentence in the passage. It is a fact. How do you know?
   A It is the author's belief.
   B It is incorrect information.
   (C) It is something that can be seen or proved.
   D All bridges do this.

School-Home Connection
Read the passage aloud with the student. Then reread it. Work together to underline each sentence that is a fact and circle each sentence that is an opinion.

Practice Book
© Harcourt • Grade 3

46

▲ Find and circle the ten compound words in the story. Write each one in the box below the story. Use a line to separate the compound word into two smaller words.

My Vacation

This summer, my family visited a waterside cottage at the beach. We could watch oceangoing steamships pass right by. I spent hours exploring the beach, and I found dozens of beautiful seashells.

Mom took sunrise walks every day, while my brother tried to ride a surfboard. He did not get very far! Dad spent time in a rowboat. He would drop his line into the water and wait for the fish to bite.

We only stayed indoors during thunderstorms. Then we would just watch the lightning, listen to the thunder, and wait to go outside again.

water | side	ocean | going
steam | ships	sea | shells
sun | rise	surf | board
row | boat	in | doors
thunder | storms	out | side

School-Home Connection
Ask the student to explain how he or she knew which words in the paragraph were compound words.

Practice Book
© Harcourt • Grade 3

47

Name _____

▲ Choose a Vocabulary Word to complete each
sentence. Write the word on the line.

| collapses | dazed | elevated |
| embarrass | midst | shabby |

1. Maya was in the ___midst___ of a large crowd of people.

2. The ___shabby___ shirt was too old to wear any longer.

3. Alejandro felt ___dazed___ after the ball hit his head.

4. The television was ___elevated___ so that everyone could
watch it.

5. Do kind words and compliments ___embarrass___ you?

6. Someone should repair that building before it ___collapses___

▲ Find a Vocabulary Word in the box below with a meaning that
matches the set of three words. Write the Vocabulary Word on
the line.

| collapses | dazed | elevated |
| embarrass | midst | shabby |

7. confused   foggy   dazzled   ___dazed___

8. raised   top   high   ___elevated___

9. topples   crashes   falls   ___collapses___

10. ragged   torn   old   ___shabby___

11. center   core   middle   ___midst___

12. shame   disgrace   upset   ___embarrass___

Name _____

▲ Use the graphic organizer to record the facts and
opinions from these pages of "The Babe and I."
Write each fact in the column labeled **Fact**. Write
each opinion in the column labeled **Opinion**.

Section 1 page 162

| Fact | Opinion |
| It was 1932, in the midst of the Great Depression, and millions of people were out of work. | We were lucky. |

Section 2 page 163–166

| Fact | Opinion |
| Babe Ruth hits home run! | Babe Ruth, the world's greatest baseball player. |

Section 3 page 167–174

| Fact | Opinion |
| Babe Ruth collapses. | Jacob was smart. |

Section 4 page 180–181

| Fact | Opinion |
| Babe Ruth was part of the 1932 Yankees. | I think the Red Sox pitcher was afraid Babe Ruth would hit a home run. |

▲ On a separate sheet of paper, summarize the story with three facts
and three opinions. Use the graphic organizer to help you.
Answers will vary.

Left Page

Name _____

Synonyms and Antonyms
Lesson 6

▲ Read each sentence and the words under it.
Circle the synonym for the underlined word.

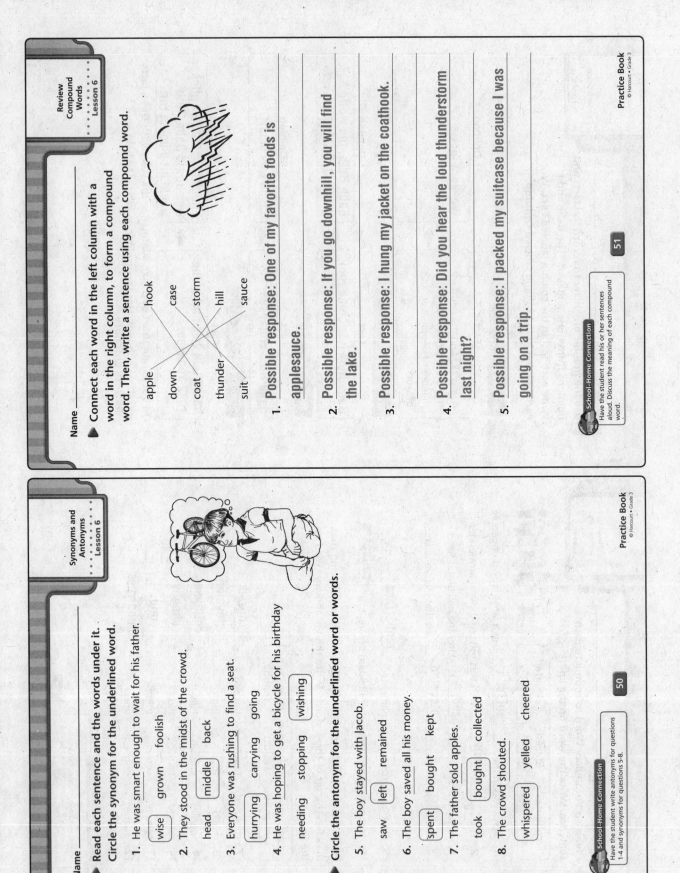

1. He was smart enough to wait for his father.
   (wise)   grown   foolish

2. They stood in the midst of the crowd.
   head   (middle)   back

3. Everyone was rushing to find a seat.
   (hurrying)   carrying   going

4. He was hoping to get a bicycle for his birthday
   needing   stopping   (wishing)

▲ Circle the antonym for the underlined word or words.

5. The boy stayed with Jacob.
   saw   (left)   remained

6. The boy saved all his money.
   (spent)   bought   kept

7. The father sold apples.
   took   (bought)   collected

8. The crowd shouted.
   (whispered)   yelled   cheered

School-Home Connection
Have the student write antonyms for questions 1–4 and synonyms for questions 5–8.

50

Practice Book
© Harcourt • Grade 3

Right Page

Name _____

Review Compound Words
Lesson 6

▲ Connect each word in the left column with a word in the right column, to form a compound word. Then, write a sentence using each compound word.

apple — sauce
down — hill
coat — hook
thunder — storm
suit — case

1. Possible response: One of my favorite foods is applesauce.

2. Possible response: If you go downhill, you will find the lake.

3. Possible response: I hung my jacket on the coathook.

4. Possible response: Did you hear the loud thunderstorm last night?

5. Possible response: I packed my suitcase because I was going on a trip.

School-Home Connection
Have the student read his or her sentences aloud. Discuss the meaning of each compound word.

51

Practice Book
© Harcourt • Grade 3

© Harcourt • Grade 3

28

Student Edition pp. 50–51

Simple and Compound Sentences
Lesson 6

Name _____

▲ Rewrite the sentences. Use commas and joining words correctly.

1. My father is a teacher and he works at a school.

    My father is a teacher, and he works at a school.

2. He drives to work, he takes a bus.

    He drives to work, or he takes a bus.

3. He has lunch at work or he eats in the park.

    He has lunch at work, or he eats in the park.

4. Most days he eats tuna, today he eats egg salad.

    Most days he eats tuna, but today he eats egg salad.

▲ Rewrite each pair of sentences as one sentence. Use commas and the joining words *and* or *but* correctly.

5. Mrs. Lopez loves to read. She owns a bookstore.

    Mrs. Lopez loves to read, and she owns a bookstore.

6. The store is small. It has many books.

    The store is small, but it has many books.

7. Sasha works with animals. She enjoys her job.

    Sasha works with animals, and she enjoys her job.

8. She lives in the country. She works in the city.

    She lives in the country, but she works in the city.

School-Home Connection

Work with your child to write two simple sentences about a person and his or her job. Then help your child turn the sentences into one compound sentence.

Practice Book
© Harcourt • Grade 3

Consonant Digraphs /ch/ch, tch; /sh/sh; /(h)w/ wh
Lesson 7

Name _____

Spelling Words
1. chin
2. itch
3. push
4. chef
5. when
6. wash
7. much
8. sharp
9. pitch
10. where
11. peach
12. child
13. wheat
14. chance
15. machine

▲ Read the Spelling Words. Find the consonants *ch, tch, sh,* or *wh* in each word. Write each word below where it belongs. **Order may vary.**

ch, wh, sh at the Beginning

1. chin
2. chef
3. when
4. sharp
5. where
6. child
7. wheat
8. chance

ch in the Middle

9. machine

sh, ch, tch at the End

10. itch
11. push
12. wash
13. much
14. pitch
15. peach

School-Home Connection

Challenge your child to write as many words with the consonant digraphs *sh, wh, ch,* and *tch* as possible. Confirm each spelling with your child by using a print or online dictionary.

Practice Book
© Harcourt • Grade 3

Name _____

▲ Read the passage below. Then answer the questions that follow.

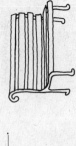

If you ever visit Africa, you might see a gorilla. Gorillas live in rain forests, mountain slopes, and bamboo forests. They live in groups as small as five or as large as thirty. A group of gorillas is called a "troop". Gorillas look fierce, but they are usually very gentle. They are big eaters — they can eat up to forty pounds of plants a day!

Sadly, gorillas are in danger. Logging companies cut down forests where gorillas live, leaving them homeless. It is sad to imagine gorillas with no place to live. Some people are trying to create new wildlife laws to protect gorillas. It is hard work, but saving gorillas is an important cause.

1. What is one opinion from the passage?
   Possible response: It is sad to imagine gorillas with no

   place to live.

2. What is one fact from the passage?
   Possible response: A group of gorillas is called a "troop".

3. What is another opinion from the passage?
   Possible response: It is hard work, but saving gorillas is

   an important cause.

School-Home Connection
Ask the student to tell you one opinion about his or her favorite animal.

54

Name _____

▲ Complete each sentence with a /ch/ word spelled ch or tch. Write the word on the line. See the word box if you need help. **Possible responses are shown.**

chance	watch	peach	hatched
bench	chin	pitch	children

1. Something you wear on your wrist that tells time is a _____.
   watch

2. If you have a group of more than one young person, you have a group of _____.
   children

3. When the bird came out of the egg, the egg was _____.
   hatched

4. In a baseball game, you _____ the ball to the batter.
   pitch

5. You may want to sit on the park _____ and rest a while.
   bench

6. A fuzzy fruit that grows on trees is a _____.
   peach

7. An opportunity is a _____ you take.
   chance

8. The part of your face just below your mouth is your _____.
   chin

School-Home Connection
Give the student four examples of words that have the /ch/ sound. Then have him or her give four more examples.

55

Name _____

▲ Read each question, paying special attention to the Vocabulary Word in dark type. Then circle the letter of the best answer.

1. How can a dog **obey** its owner?
   Ⓐ By following the owner's commands
   B By doing the opposite of what the owner asks
   C By barking at other dogs

2. What sound would a child make if he or she **whined**?
   A A happy sound
   Ⓑ A complaining sound
   C A playful sound

3. What can give off a pleasant **scent**?
   A A skunk
   B A pile of garbage
   Ⓒ A bed of flowers

4. How can you **demonstrate** the way to set a table?
   A Tell someone what to do.
   B Ask someone to show you how to do it.
   Ⓒ Do it yourself while someone is watching.

5. What does someone do who **wanders** about?
   Ⓐ Walks without a plan
   B Talks on the phone for hours
   C Writes a long letter

6. Why would someone **patrol** a neighborhood?
   A To water the plants
   Ⓑ To keep it safe
   C To keep it crowded

School–Home Connection
Have the student use each Vocabulary Word in an original sentence.

Name _____

▲ As you read "Aero and Officer Mike," fill in the graphic organizer with facts and opinions from the passage. Possible responses are shown.

Section 1 pages 200–209

Fact	Opinion
• Aero is a black and tan German shepherd.	• Aero likes the words "Good Dog!"
• Officer Mike has a special car for Aero.	

Section 2 pages 210–215

• Aero can run about forty miles an hour.	• Aero likes children.
	• Both Aero and Officer Mike love being police officers.

1. What is a fact about Aero's training?
   Possible response: Officer Mike can communicate with Aero using hand signals.

2. How does Aero feel about steep stairs and open gratings? He does not like them; he is scared of them.

▲ On a separate sheet of paper, summarize the selection. Use the graphic organizer to help you.

Synonyms and Antonyms
Lesson 7

Name _____

▲ Write a synonym or antonym for the underlined word in each sentence.
Possible answers are shown.

1. Kim had to <u>jump</u> to reach the top shelf of her closet.

   Synonym: _____ leap

2. I cannot see <u>over</u> the table from where I am sitting.

   Antonym: _____ under

3. Joe thought that last night's show was <u>awful</u>.

   Synonym: _____ terrible

4. You can keep any of the <u>objects</u> in this box.

   Synonym: _____ things

5. Those books are <u>heavy</u>.

   Antonym: _____ light

6. The ranger's cabin is in the <u>woods</u>.

   Synonym: _____ forest

7. <u>Everybody</u> wants to go to the movies tonight.

   Antonym: _____ nobody

8. The dog's <u>hair</u> is brown.

   Synonym: _____ fur

School-Home Connection
Ask the student to think of two antonyms for item #3.

58

Practice Book
© Harcourt • Grade 3

Consonant Digraphs: ch, sh, /(h)w/wh
Lesson 7

Name _____

▲ Circle the word with the consonant pattern that is not pronounced like the other two.

1. chin   march   (chef)

2. when   why   (who)

3. (chubby)   cash   machine

4. child   (sharp)   chance

5. write   wrist   (wheat)

6. (push)   pitch   chap

7. shake   shoot   (chase)

8. stitch   (whale)   catch

9. much   patch   (wheel)

10. (short)   chat   chart

School-Home Connection
With the student, write four sentences that use at least one word each with consonant patterns ch, tch, sh, and wh.

59

Practice Book
© Harcourt • Grade 3

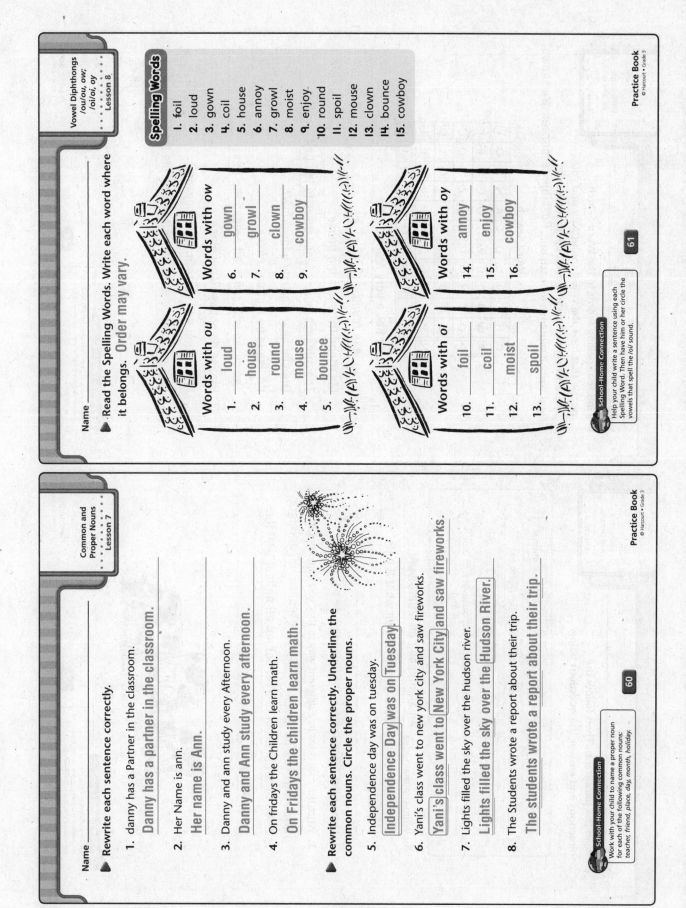

Common and Proper Nouns
Lesson 7

Name _____

▲ Rewrite each sentence correctly.

1. danny has a Partner in the classroom.
   Danny has a partner in the classroom.

2. Her Name is ann.
   Her name is Ann.

3. Danny and ann study every Afternoon.
   Danny and Ann study every afternoon.

4. On fridays the Children learn math.
   On Fridays the children learn math.

▲ Rewrite each sentence correctly. Underline the common nouns. Circle the proper nouns.

5. Independence day was on tuesday.
   Independence Day was on Tuesday.

6. Yani's class went to new york city and saw fireworks.
   Yani's class went to New York City and saw fireworks.

7. Lights filled the sky over the hudson river.
   Lights filled the sky over the Hudson River.

8. The Students wrote a report about their trip.
   The students wrote a report about their trip.

School-Home Connection
Work with your child to name a proper noun for each of the following common nouns: teacher, friend, place, day, month, holiday.

Practice Book
© Harcourt • Grade 3

60

Vowel Diphthongs
/ou/ou, ow;
/oi/oi, oy
Lesson 8

Spelling Words
1. foil
2. loud
3. gown
4. coil
5. house
6. annoy
7. growl
8. moist
9. enjoy
10. round
11. spoil
12. mouse
13. clown
14. bounce
15. cowboy

Name _____

▲ Read the Spelling Words. Write each word where it belongs. Order may vary.

Words with ou
1. loud
2. house
3. round
4. mouse
5. bounce

Words with ow
6. gown
7. growl
8. clown
9. cowboy

Words with oi
10. foil
11. coil
12. moist
13. spoil

Words with oy
14. annoy
15. enjoy
16. cowboy

School-Home Connection
Help your child write a sentence using each Spelling Word. Then have him or her circle the vowels that spell the /oi/ sound.

Practice Book
© Harcourt • Grade 3

61

33

Student Edition pp. 60–61

Name _____

▲ Read the paragraph. Then follow the
directions and answer the questions below.

> Did you know that rabbits eat only plants? This type of animal
> is called a herbivore. Animals that are carnivores, like tigers, eat only
> meat. Some animals, like bears, eat both plants and meat. They are
> called omnivores. An animal can be a herbivore, carnivore, or omnivore
> depending on what it eats.

1. Write the main idea. An animal can be a herbivore,
   carnivore, or omnivore depending on what it eats.

2. Draw a box around each of the supporting details.

3. Write the main idea in a different way so that you could put it at the
   beginning of the paragraph. Possible response: All animals
   need to eat in order to live, but not all animals eat the
   same thing.

62

Practice Book
© Harcourt • Grade 3

Name _____

▲ Find ten spelling words in the Word Search
puzzle that have the vowel sound /ou/ and /oi/.
The words go across or down. Circle the words
and write a sentence for each one. Possible responses are shown.

Word Search

C	H	L	O	U	D	T	A	N	N	O	Y
R	W	N	D	G	W	O	O	C	Y	F	L
O	Q	K	H	O	U	S	E	Z	T	O	C
U	G	R	O	W	L	X	R	U	Q	I	O
N	P	C	M	N	O	Y	X	L	X	L	I
D	C	L	O	W	N	O	S	P	O	I	L

1. My sister has a very *loud* voice.

2. A circle is *round*.

3. My friend lives in a big *house*.

4. The princess wore a fancy *gown* to the ball.

5. Did you hear a grizzly bear *growl*?

6. I'd like to be a circus *clown*.

7. The snake will *coil* itself around the tree.

8. Please do not *spoil* my niece.

9. My brother will sometimes *annoy* me.

10. Will you please wrap the *foil* around the food?

63

Practice Book
© Harcourt • Grade 3

Name

▲ **Part A.** Write the Vocabulary Word from the Word Box that matches each idea.

| communicate | flick | alert |
| signal | chatter | grooms |

1. <u>grooms</u>   to make neat and clean

2. <u>communicate</u>   to tell a person or animal something

3. <u>alert</u>   to warn someone

4. <u>chatter</u>   to make noises over and over

5. <u>signal</u>   a movement that has a meaning

6. <u>flick</u>   to snap something quickly

▲ **Part B.** Use what you know about the Vocabulary Words to answer each question. Answer in complete sentences. **Possible responses are shown.**

7. If you **alert** someone, are you smiling at the person or warning the person? **You are warning the person.**

8. If you **flick** a towel, does the towel move quickly or slowly? **The towel moves quickly.**

9. If a person **grooms** his dog, is he brushing it or feeding it? **He is brushing the dog.**

10. If you **chatter** with a friend, are you speaking quickly or whispering? **You are speaking quickly.**

11. When you give someone a **signal**, what are you doing? **You are giving the person a message.**

12. Do you **communicate** by yourself or with other people? **You communicate with other people.**

School-Home Connection
Have the student act out the words alert and chatter. Then use your hands to send a signal to him or her. Have the student guess what the signal means.

Name

▲ As you read "How Animals Talk," fill in the graphic organizer with important details from the selection. Then write the most important idea from the selection. **Possible responses are shown.**

Main Idea

Detail
Some animals send messages with sounds.

Detail

Detail

1. What is the main idea of the selection?
   <u>Animals have many different ways of communicating.</u>

2. What are three of the most important details?
   <u>Answers will vary but should support the main idea.</u>

▲ On a separate sheet of paper, summarize the selection. Use the graphic organizer to help you. **Answers will vary.**

Name _____

▲ Read the encyclopedia entry. Use the information to answer the questions.

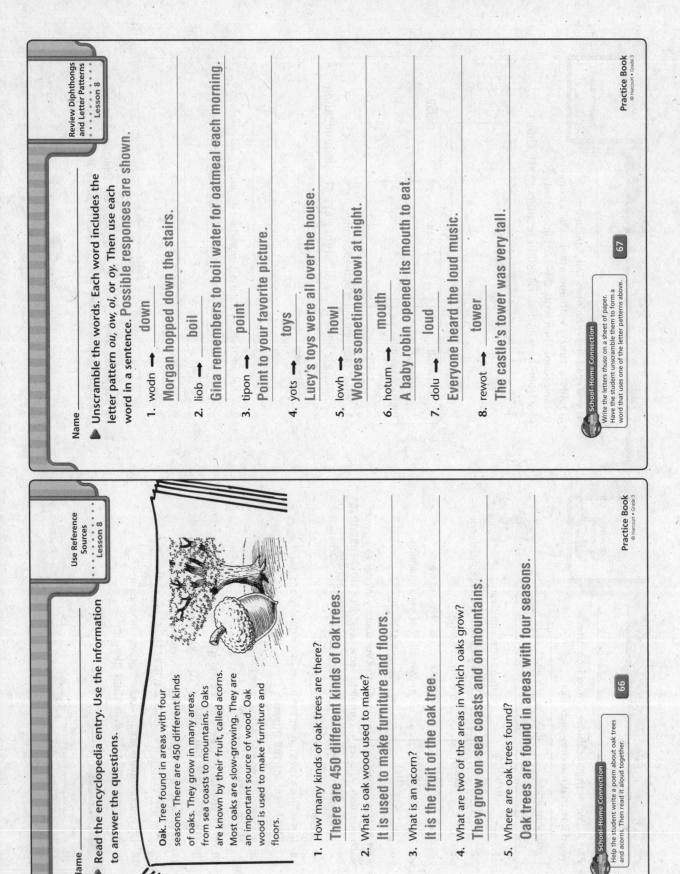

Oak. Tree found in areas with four seasons. There are 450 different kinds of oaks. They grow in many areas, from sea coasts to mountains. Oaks are known by their fruit, called acorns. Most oaks are slow-growing. They are an important source of wood. Oak wood is used to make furniture and floors.

1. How many kinds of oak trees are there?
   There are 450 different kinds of oak trees.

2. What is oak wood used to make?
   It is used to make furniture and floors.

3. What is an acorn?
   It is the fruit of the oak tree.

4. What are two of the areas in which oaks grow?
   They grow on sea coasts and on mountains.

5. Where are oak trees found?
   Oak trees are found in areas with four seasons.

School-Home Connection

Help the student write a poem about oak trees and acorns. Then read it aloud together.

Name _____

▲ Unscramble the words. Each word includes the letter pattern *ou*, *ow*, *oi*, or *oy*. Then use each word in a sentence. Possible responses are shown.

1. wodn → down
   Morgan hopped down the stairs.

2. liob → boil
   Gina remembers to boil water for oatmeal each morning.

3. tipon → point
   Point to your favorite picture.

4. yots → toys
   Lucy's toys were all over the house.

5. lowh → howl
   Wolves sometimes howl at night.

6. hotum → mouth
   A baby robin opened its mouth to eat.

7. dolu → loud
   Everyone heard the loud music.

8. rewot → tower
   The castle's tower was very tall.

School-Home Connection

Write the letters *thuso* on a sheet of paper. Have the student unscramble them to form a word that uses one of the letter patterns above.

Abbreviations
Lesson 8

Name _____

▲ Write the full word for each abbreviation.

1. FL   **Florida**

2. Tues.   **Tuesday**

3. Dr.   **Doctor**

4. St.   **Street**

5. Apr.   **April**

▲ Find the words in each sentence that have abbreviations. Write the abbreviations.

6. Mister Ward's party is on Sunday, November 5.
   Mr., Sun., Nov.

7. Send the letter to Doctor Johnson at 5 Mesa Street, El Paso, Texas.
   Dr., St., TX

8. In September, Mistress Torres's class goes to the animal shelter on River Avenue.
   Sept., Mrs., Ave.

9. Tennessee and Missouri are next to Kentucky.
   TN, MO, KY

10. Mistress Brecht spoke at the school on Barstow Road on Friday.
    Mrs., Rd., Fri.

Practice Book
© Harcourt • Grade 3

Consonant Blends
str, scr, spr
Lesson 9

Name _____

Spelling Words

1. spray
2. street
3. sprint
4. stripe
5. screen
6. strong
7. spring
8. stray
9. scream
10. strike
11. spread
12. string
13. sprout
14. scratch
15. stream

▲ Read the Spelling Words. Write each word where it belongs. **Order may vary.**

Words with str

1. street
2. stripe
3. strong
4. stray
5. strike
6. string
7. stream

Words with scr

8. screen
9. scream
10. scratch

Words with spr

11. spray
12. sprint
13. spring
14. spread
15. sprout

Practice Book
© Harcourt • Grade 3

Student Edition pp. 68–69

Left page

▲ Read the passage. Then circle the letter of the best answer to each question.

Did you ever trade one thing for another? It can be fun. It also is a good way to get rid of old things and find yourself some wonderful new treasures. People have been swapping things for thousands of years. In ancient times, money was hard to get. So one family would trade their extra cow for another family's extra pig or horse. Today, people get most of what they need by buying things in stores. But swapping and trading is still going on. You can swap books with a friend. That way, you can trade a book you have read for a book that will be new and exciting to you. You can do the same thing with toys, games, and clothes that no longer fit.

Tip
Remember that details help explain the main idea.

1. What is the main idea of the passage?
   A It's fun!
   Ⓑ Swapping is a great way to trade old things for new treasures.
   C You can swap books with a friend.

2. Which detail does not support the main idea?
   A Swapping and trading is still going on.
   B In ancient times, money was hard to get.
   Ⓒ It's a nice day.

3. Which detail supports the main idea?
   Ⓐ You can swap books with a friend.
   B The word *paws* spelled backwards is *swap*.
   C Books can be a great deal of fun.

School-Home Connection
Reread the passage with the student. Then have the student retell the main idea in his or her own words.

70

Practice Book
© Harcourt • Grade 3

© Harcourt • Grade 3

Right page

▲ Make real words by adding *str* or *scr* to the endings in the box. Then write each finished word under the correct heading.

str	scr

eet   oke   ap   atch   ing   eak   ape   eam

str words
street
stroke
strap
string
streak
stream

scr words
scrap
scratch
scrape
scream

School-Home Connection
Ask the student to blend *str* and *scr* with the ending *-ub*. Have him or her tell you which combination makes a real word and which makes a nonsense word.

71

Practice Book
© Harcourt • Grade 3

Name

▲ **Choose the correct Vocabulary Word from the box to answer each riddle.**

| banquet | agreeable | curiosity |
| gaze | famine | generous |

1. I am quite unusual. You might find me if you hunt through old treasure chests. I am a ___curiosity___

2. I can be great fun. I have a lot of delicious food, and you might have to get dressed in fancy clothes. I am a ___banquet___

3. I will not make you sick or unhappy. In fact, you will not find anything wrong with me at all. I am ___agreeable___

4. I look at you as though you are the most interesting thing in the world. I ___gaze___ at you.

5. I will give you everything I have and more. I am ___generous___

6. When I am around, people feel very hungry. I am a ___famine___

▲ **Now it's your turn. Write riddles for the two Vocabulary Words below. Answers will vary.**

banquet   generous

7. _____

8. _____

School-Home Connection
Play charades with the student. Take turns giving clues to guess each Vocabulary Word.

Name

▲ As you read "Stone Soup," answer the questions below, and fill in the graphic organizer with the main idea and important details. **Possible responses are shown.**

1. What is the main idea of the story? Put it in the Main Idea box.

2. What is one important detail on page 258? Put it in the first Detail box.

3. What is one important detail on page 261? Put it in the second Detail box.

4. What is one important detail on page 271? Put it in the last Detail box.

Main Idea: Sharing brings happiness.

Detail: (p. 258)
Three monks want to find out what makes people happy.

Detail: (p. 261)
As each villager gives, others want to give more.

Detail: (p. 271)
A villager says, "To be happy is as simple as making stone soup."

▲ Use the information from the graphic organizer above to write a summary of the story on a separate sheet of paper.

▲ Look up each word in a thesaurus. Write two synonyms for the word. **Answers will vary.**

1. make _____ create _____ build

   Synonyms:

2. walk _____ hike _____ stroll

   Synonyms:

3. sleepy _____ tired _____ drowsy

   Synonyms:

4. angry _____ mad _____ furious

   Synonyms:

5. leader _____ boss _____ guide

   Synonyms:

6. friend _____ pal _____ buddy

   Synonyms:

School-Home Connection

Have the student name three feelings, such as *happy*, *sad*, and *nervous*. Help him or her find synonyms for these words in a thesaurus.

▲ Combine letters to make words that have 3 consonants in a row. Start each word with letters from Row 1. End the word with letters from Row 2. The first one has been done for you.

Row 1

st   trans   hun   com   sub   cen   spr   sc   sp   str

Row 2

tral   roller   inkle   tract   ramble   plete   dred   form   read   eam

1. _____ stroller

2. _____ transform

3. _____ hundred

4. _____ complete

5. _____ subtract

6. _____ central

7. _____ sprinkle

8. _____ scramble

9. _____ spread

10. _____ stream

School-Home Connection

Ask the student to choose three of these words and use them in sentences.

Name _____

▲ Write the correct plural form of each singular noun. Use a dictionary if you need to.

1. pot   pots
2. raspberry   raspberries
3. tomato   tomatoes
4. meal   meals
5. rabbit   rabbits
6. moose   moose
7. sheep   sheep
8. puppy   puppies

▲ Rewrite the sentences. Use the plural forms of the nouns in parentheses ( ). Use a dictionary if you need to.

9. The (child) made (sandwich).
   The children made sandwiches.

10. Amber sliced (carrot) and (apple).
    Amber sliced carrots and apples.

11. Do you want (blueberry) or (peach)?
    Do you want blueberries or peaches?

12. Brush your (tooth) after you eat the (strawberry).
    Brush your teeth after you eat the strawberries.

Name _____

▲ Write a compound word for each meaning. Combine words from the box to make the compounds.

flower	street	snow	bath	suit
rain	coat	sun	block	light	pot
		star	fish	bird	

1. An outside lamp   streetlight
2. A child's winter clothing   snowsuit
3. A five-pointed sea creature   starfish
4. A container for growing plants   flowerpot
5. A kind of lotion you put on your skin in the summer   sunblock
6. A place where robins go to clean their feathers   birdbath
7. A piece of clothing you wear to keep yourself dry   raincoat

Name _____

▲ Fold the paper along the dotted line. As each spelling word is read aloud, write it in the blank. Then unfold your paper and check your work. Practice writing any spelling words you missed.

Spelling Words

1. airplane
2. upstairs
3. something
4. itch
5. chef
6. wheat
7. chance
8. push
9. enjoy
10. moist
11. clown
12. loud
13. sprint
14. street
15. scratch

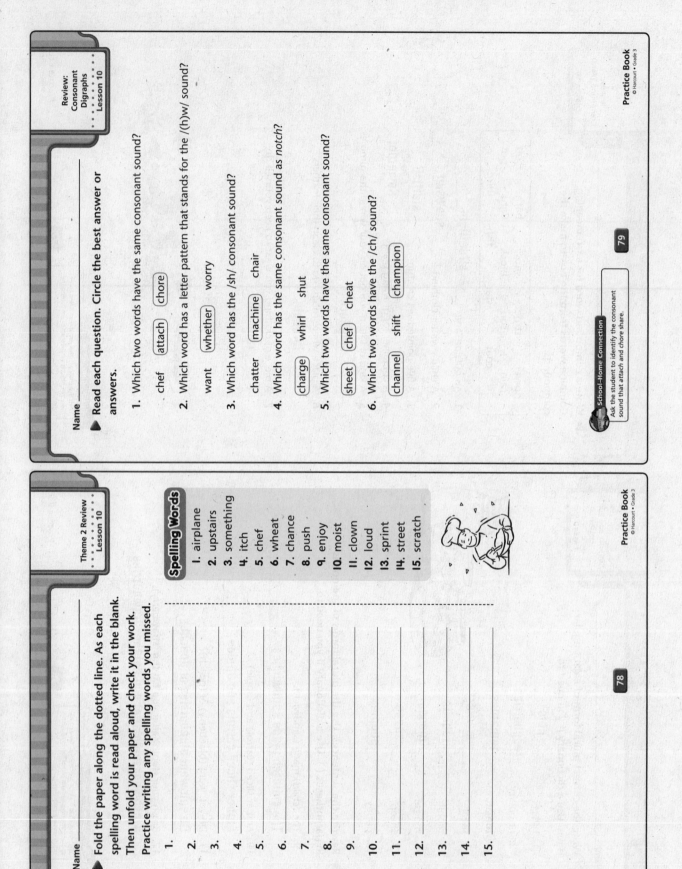

1. _____
2. _____
3. _____
4. _____
5. _____
6. _____
7. _____
8. _____
9. _____
10. _____
11. _____
12. _____
13. _____
14. _____
15. _____

Name _____

▲ Read each question. Circle the best answer or answers.

1. Which two words have the same consonant sound?

   chef   (attach)   (chore)

2. Which word has a letter pattern that stands for the /(h)w/ sound?

   want   (whether)   worry

3. Which word has the /sh/ consonant sound?

   chatter   (machine)   chair

4. Which word has the same consonant sound as *notch*?

   (charge)   whirl   shut

5. Which two words have the same consonant sound?

   (sheet)   (chef)   cheat

6. Which two words have the /ch/ sound?

   (channel)   shift   (champion)

School-Home Connection
Ask the student to identify the consonant sound that *attach* and *chore* share.

Review: Fact and Opinion
Lesson 10

▲ **Read the selection below. Then answer the questions.**

I love to paint with bright colors. Colors are so interesting! Did you know that just three colors make up almost all the different colors we see? Red, blue, and yellow combine to make many other colors. For example, red and blue make purple. Yellow and red make orange. Yellow and blue make green. And with these colors, a painter can make new colors. Paintings with lots of colors are the most beautiful kind. What kind of paintings do you like?

1. Write two facts from the passage.
Possible response: Red and blue make purple; Yellow and red make orange.

2. Write two opinions from the passage.
Possible response: Colors are so interesting! Paintings with lots of colors are the most beautiful kind.

3. Answer the question in the last sentence of the passage, giving your opinion.
Accept all reasonable responses.

School-Home Connection
Ask the student to describe a sunset, using both facts and opinions.

Grammar–Writing
Connection
Lesson 10

▲ **Read this part of a student's rough draft. Then answer the questions that follow.**

(1) Mrs. Sanchez's class performed a play on _____, October 2. (2) The Play was at the Madison Elementary School. (3) At 7:00 P.M. (4) My sister Elaine acted, she did a great job. (5) My bedtime is 8:00 P.M. (6) My parents let me stay up late to watch the play.

1. Which word could go in the blank in Sentence 1?
Ⓐ Monday
B tuesday
C evening
D lunchtime

2. Which word in Sentence 2 is incorrectly capitalized?
Ⓐ Play
B Madison
C Elementary
D School

3. Which word should follow the comma in Sentence 4?
A but
B or
Ⓒ and
D tonight

4. Which is the proper noun in Sentence 4?
A sister
Ⓑ Elaine
C great
D job

5. Which two simple sentences could be joined by a comma followed by *but*?
A Sentences 1 and 2
B Sentences 3 and 4
C Sentences 4 and 5
Ⓓ Sentences 5 and 6

6. Which sentence is NOT complete?
A Sentence 2
Ⓑ Sentence 3
C Sentence 5
D Sentence 6

▲ **Read each sentence. Complete each unfinished word by writing ou, ow, oi, or oy on the blanks.**

1. I do not like brussels spr __ o __ __ u __ ts.

2. What time is your doctor's app __ o __ __ i __ ntment?

3. Try not to ann __ o __ __ y __ your little brother.

4. What do you think pigs are saying when they __ o __ __ i __ nk?

5. The five v __ o __ __ w __ els are a, e, i, o, and u.

6. Albert added fl __ o __ __ u __ r to the bread dough.

7. My mother enj __ o __ __ y __ s gardening.

8. Be careful not to confuse baking soda with baking p __ o __ __ w __ der.

▲ **Write a synonym or an antonym for the underlined word in each sentence.** Possible responses are shown.

Synonyms

1. It was a dark, chilly night. ___cold___

2. Please throw me the ball. ___toss___

3. We were wet from head to toe. ___soaked___

4. What a wonderful time we had! ___great___

5. Gregg is kind to his Aunt. ___friendly___

Antonyms

6. The dog's bowl was empty. ___full___

7. We took the crooked path. ___straight___

8. I think I made a huge mistake. ___tiny___

9. We were all bored by the play. ___excited___

10. He was an excellent teacher. ___bad___

© Harcourt • Grade 3

Name _____

▲ Part A. Complete each sentence with one of the Vocabulary Words from the Word Box.

| investigate | laboratory | suspect |
| expert | various | confess |

1. Every night, the scientists wash all the beakers in the **laboratory**

2. When her parents found the flashlight under her pillow, Leigh had to **confess** she had been staying up past her bedtime to read.

3. I **suspect** you will not like the reptile documentary since you are afraid of snakes.

4. Tomorrow, Dad and I will go to the store to **investigate** the best kind of food processor to buy.

5. Santino is good at kickball, but he is certainly not an **expert** at the game.

6. This summer, I read **various** books about mice.

▲ Part B. Write a sentence describing something you might investigate in a laboratory.

Possible response: I would like to investigate what happens when you mix baking soda and vinegar.

84

Practice Book
© Harcourt • Grade 3

Name _____

▲ Part A. Draw a line from each consonant blend in Column A to four different letter groups in Column B to form words.

Column A   Column B

eech
amble
ide
ict
scr   ape
ay
str   uggle
atch

▲ Part B.

1. Which letter combination from Column B will make a word with the consonant blend *spr*? **ay**

2. Use this new word in a sentence:

Possible response: If you spray the dough with water, it will not dry out in the oven.

85

Practice Book
© Harcourt • Grade 3

▲ Read this part of a student's rough draft.
Then answer the questions that follow.

(1) There is a mystery to solve at 10 Mountain Road.
(2) The Brooks children can't find their puppy. (3) What
are the clue? (4) The door is open, and cookies are baking
in the house across the street. (5) _____ Brooks says she
knows where the puppy is. (6) Do you?

1. What is the abbreviation for
the underlined word in
Sentence 1?

A rd
B rd.
C Rd.
D RD

2. What is the correct plural form
of the noun in Sentence 3?

A clue
B clues
C cluees
D cluies

3. How many SINGULAR nouns
are in Sentence 4?

A two
B three
C four
D five

4. How many PLURAL nouns are
in Sentence 4?

A one
B two
C three
D four

5. Which abbreviation could go
in the blank in Sentence 5?

A mrs
B Mrs
C MS
D Mrs.

6. Which sentence has an
irregular plural noun?

A Sentence 2
B Sentence 3
C Sentence 4
D Sentence 5

Practice Book
© Harcourt • Grade 3

▲ Read the selection. Write an answer to each
question. Possible responses are shown.

My class is taking a field trip to a campground next week. I am very
excited because we are going to learn how to set up a tent. If the weather
is nice, we can even start a fire and roast some marshmallows. We will
leave for the trip at 8 A.M. and get to the campsite by 10 A.M. I have a
new book to read on the bus. Our teacher will show us how to identify
poison ivy and other plants in the woods. The trip
will teach us about nature and what it is like to
live without many things from the modern world.

1. What is the main idea of the passage?
My class is taking a field trip to a campground.

2. What are two supporting details in the passage?
We are going to learn how to set up a tent; we will leave
at 8 a.m.

3. What is a detail that does not support the main idea?
I have a new book to read on the bus.

School–Home Connection
Ask the student to identify another sentence
that tells the main idea of the selection.

Practice Book
© Harcourt • Grade 3

© Harcourt • Grade 3

Student Edition pp. 86–87

Review: Use Reference Sources — Lesson 10

Name _____

▲ Write the answer to each question.

Reference Sources
dictionary   encyclopedia
thesaurus   atlas

1. Which reference source would you use to find a synonym for *empty?* ____thesaurus____

2. Which reference source would you use to find out which countries border Panama? ____atlas____

3. Which reference source tells what *lilac* means? ____dictionary____

4. Which reference source describes the climate in which palm trees grow and how long it takes them to grow? ____encyclopedia____

5. Which reference source would you use to find an antonym for *pleasant?* ____thesaurus____

School-Home Connection
Ask the student to name three types of information found in a dictionary.

88

Practice Book
© Harcourt • Grade 3

Consonant -le Syllable Pattern — Lesson 11

Name _____

Spelling Words
1. title
2. table
3. uncle
4. apple
5. cable
6. bubble
7. beetle
8. rattle
9. purple
10. little
11. middle
12. simple
13. saddle
14. trouble
15. scribble

▲ Read the Spelling Words. Then read the name of each group. Write each word where it belongs. **Order may vary.**

Words with *ble*

1. table
2. cable
3. bubble
4. trouble
5. scribble

Words with *dle*

6. middle   7. saddle

Word with *cle*

8. uncle

Words with *ple*

9. apple
10. purple
11. simple

Words with *tle*

12. title   14. beetle
13. rattle   15. little

School-Home Connection
Help your child write several words that rhyme with *cable*, *little*, and *bubble*. Discuss the correct spelling of each word. Confirm each word's spelling using a print or an online dictionary.

89

Practice Book
© Harcourt • Grade 3

▲ Circle the C-*le* word and use it in a sentence.
Possible sentences are shown.

1. [staple] stapel stapple
   I needed to *staple* the pages together.

2. muble [mumble] mummble
   It is hard to hear people when they *mumble*.

3. ridel ridle [riddle]
   My friend asked me a funny *riddle*.

4. starttle [startle] gentle
   You should not *startle* an animal.

5. padel [paddle] paddoul
   You can *paddle* a canoe across the lake.

6. genttle genle [gentle]
   Rabbits are very *gentle* animals.

7. [cable] cabble cabel
   The steel *cable* was eight feet long.

8. titel [title] titel
   The *title* of the book was difficult to read.

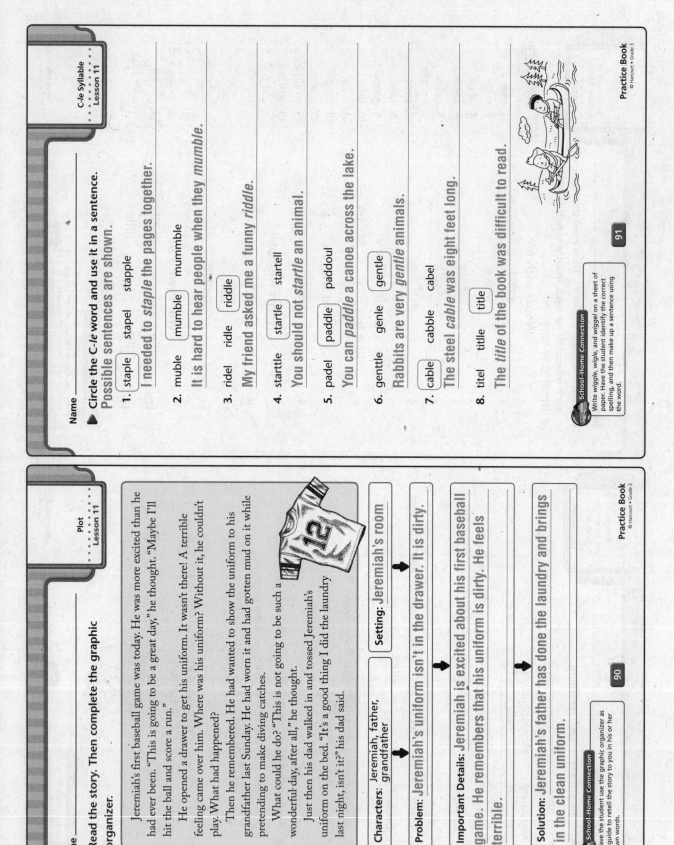

▲ Read the story. Then complete the graphic organizer.

Jeremiah's first baseball game was today. He was more excited than he had ever been. "This is going to be a great day," he thought. "Maybe I'll hit the ball and score a run."

He opened a drawer to get his uniform. It wasn't there! A terrible feeling came over him. Where was his uniform? Without it, he couldn't play. What had happened?

Then he remembered. He had wanted to show the uniform to his grandfather last Sunday. He had worn it and had gotten mud on it while pretending to make diving catches.

What could he do? "This is not going to be such a wonderful day, after all," he thought.

Just then his dad walked in and tossed Jeremiah's uniform on the bed. "It's a good thing I did the laundry last night, isn't it?" his dad said.

Characters: Jeremiah, father, grandfather

→

Setting: Jeremiah's room

→

Problem: Jeremiah's uniform isn't in the drawer. It is dirty.

→

Important Details: Jeremiah is excited about his first baseball game. He remembers that his uniform is dirty. He feels terrible.

→

Solution: Jeremiah's father has done the laundry and brings in the clean uniform.

Name _____

▲ As you read "Loved Best," fill in the graphic organizer. Record the important facts you learn along the way.

Section 1 pages 306–308

Characters: Mrs. Lasiter, **Dana** Carolyn, Mama, Daddy, Granddaddy, **Josh, Greg Steward, Debra Miller, Grandmama**

Setting: community center

Section 2 page 312

Problem: Carolyn worries that her parents love her siblings more.

Section 3 pages 302–319

Important Events: Dana and Josh perform successfully. Carolyn is too nervous to perform. Carolyn runs from the stage. Carolyn talks to her mother in the parking lot.

Section 4 page 320

Solution: Carolyn's mother convinces her that she is loved as much as her brothers and sisters.

▲ On a separate sheet of paper, summarize the story. Use the graphic organizer to help you.

Name _____

▲ Read each question. Pay special attention to the Vocabulary Word that is underlined. Then write your answer on the line. **Answers may vary.**

1. If you sobbed at the end of a movie, how would you describe that movie to a friend?
   I would tell my friend the movie was sad.

2. If you hoped to be encouraging to a friend who was about to act in a play, what would you say?
   Good luck. You are going to do well.

3. When might you hear people chuckling?
   People may start chuckling after they hear a joke.

4. What is something you could do that would be soothing, especially after working hard?
   I could lie down on the couch and take a nap.

5. If you had a brief amount of time to eat, what would you eat?
   For a quick meal, I would eat a sandwich.

6. When has someone praised you recently?
   My mother said I did a good job when I cleaned my room.

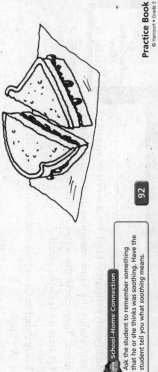

Name _____

▲ Read each sentence. Look for a word or words with about the same meaning as the underlined word. Then circle the letter of the best definition for that underlined word.

1. I grinned at Grandma, and she beamed back at me.
   (A) smiled
   B growled
   C gave an unhappy look
   D laughed loudly

2. Carolyn's nervous stomach churned, and she thought it would never stop spinning.
   A grew calm
   B turned into butter
   C enjoyed
   (D) stirred violently

3. The performance was over, and everyone had enjoyed the play.
   A the whole group
   B a happy look
   (C) show
   D meal

4. The entire class was looking at her, and all of her classmates showed concern.
   (A) whole
   B wheels of a large truck
   C small
   D best

Practice Book
© Harcourt • Grade 3

94

Name _____

▲ Write the C-le word that goes with each clue. Then cross out the two syllables in the box that make up the word you wrote. When you are done, the leftover syllables will form a word that is "easy" to read.

bee	gle	bot	ea	crum	ple
ple	dle	fid	tle	dou	ap
ble	cra	sim	tle	dle	ble

1. Another name for a violin _____ fiddle
2. A place to put a doll or a baby _____ cradle
3. To break into many pieces _____ crumble
4. A kind of insect _____ beetle
5. A container made from glass or plastic _____ bottle
6. The national bird of the United States _____ eagle
7. A kind of fruit _____ apple
8. Twice as much _____ double

The word that is "easy" to read is _____ simple

Practice Book
© Harcourt • Grade 3

95

50

© Harcourt • Grade 3

Student Edition pp. 94–95

Possessive Nouns
Lesson 11

Name _____

▲ Rewrite each phrase. Use the correct possessive noun.

1. the costumes that belong to the girls
the girls' costumes

2. the dance of Ron
Ron's dance

3. the necklace owned by her grandmother
her grandmother's necklace

4. the bottles of the babies
the babies' bottles

5. the sleeves of the dresses
the dresses' sleeves

6. the car that belongs to my mother
my mother's car

▲ Write sentences using the noun below. The words in parentheses ( ) tell which form of the noun to use. Possible responses are shown.

dancer

7. (singular) A dancer performed at school.

8. (plural) Two dancers are on stage.

9. (singular possessive) The dancer's costume is pretty.

10. (plural possessive) The dancers' legs were sore.

Practice Book
© Harcourt • Grade 3

Silent Letters
kn, gn, wr, gh
Lesson 12

Spelling Words

1. gnat
2. knew
3. sign
4. knob
5. gnaw
6. write
7. knees
8. wrinkle
9. kneel
10. wrist
11. cough
12. known
13. rough
14. wrench
15. knight

Name _____

▲ Make cards for the Spelling Words. Lay them down and read them. Order may vary.

1. Put the words that have silent letters at the beginning in one group. Then write the words in the chart.

2. Put the words that have silent letters in the middle in one group. Then write the words in the chart.

3. Put the words that have silent letters at the end in another group. Then write the words in the chart.

Beginning

1. gnat	5. write	9. wrist
2. knew	6. knees	10. known
3. knob	7. wrinkle	11. wrench
4. gnaw	8. kneel	12. knight

Middle

13. knight

14. sign

End

15. cough

16. rough

Practice Book
© Harcourt • Grade 3

Student Edition pp. 96–97

▲ Read the story. Then write answers to the questions.

Nita was walking the family dog, Abe, when a car raced by. Abe barked. Nita ran home.

"We have to make drivers slow down. These cars could hurt Abel" Nita said to her father and her older sister.

"Maybe you and your sister can write a letter to the newspaper. The paper will publish it, and a lot of people will read about the cars on our street. That may make some of them drive more slowly," said her father.

"Come on," Nita's sister, Vera, said. "We can do this together." Nita and Vera wrote the letter. The newspaper sent a reporter to do a story, and Nita and Abe had their picture in the paper! The town put up a sign on Nita's street. It read, "Please slow down. Children and pets live here. Drive slowly!" People now drive slowly down Nita's street.

1. Who is the main character?
   Nita is the main character.

2. Who are the other characters? **Nita's sister, Vera, their father,**
   the reporter and Abe are also characters.

3. What is a very important event in the story?
   A car races by Nita and Abe.

4. What problem is faced by the main character? **She wants to**
   keep speeding cars from hurting pets.

5. What is the solution to the problem?
   Nita and Vera write a letter to the newspaper. Because of
   this, a new sign is put up asking drivers to slow down.

School-Home Connection
With the student, write a letter to a newspaper about a problem in your community.

98

Practice Book
© Harcourt • Grade 3

© Harcourt • Grade 3

▲ Unscramble the underlined letters and write the word on the line.

1. A small creature that appears in old stories is a meong.
   gnome

2. Tapping on a door or a window is called gcoinnkk.
   knocking

3. Very small insects that sometimes swarm around people are stang.
   gnats

4. A brave soldier from the Middle Ages is a kingth.
   knight

5. You can make tnsok with string or rope.
   knots

6. Gary slowly turned the round nbok on the door.
   knob

7. The hungry cougar edgnwa on a tender bone.
   gnawed

8. Sharon's keens were very strong because she walked uphill every day.
   knees

9. The stop nigs was bright red.
   sign

10. Please lenke at the water's edge, and quietly watch the manatees swim.
   kneel

School-Home Connection
Have the student act out as many of the words as he or she can.

99

Practice Book
© Harcourt • Grade 3

Name _____

▲ Pick the word from the Word Box that best fits with each group of three words. Write the word on the line.

| translate | bothersome | dodging |
| din | heaving | repairs |

1. loud
crowded
yelling
din

2. annoying
pesky
disturb
bothersome

3. fix
patch
mend
repairs

4. words
change
language
translate

5. escaping
quick
diving
dodging

6. earth
moving
quaking
heaving

School–Home Connection
Have the student show you a **dodging** movement. Then have him or her imitate how a **bothersome** person might act.

Practice Book
© Harcourt • Grade 3

Name _____

▲ As you read "A Pen Pal for Max," fill in the graphic organizer with important information from the story.

Characters	Setting
Max, Don Manuel, Maggie	Small farm in Chile

PLOT

Problem
Max would like a faraway friend. Max gets a letter in English, which he cannot read. Max cannot go to school because it is closed.

Important Events
Max includes a letter in a box of grapes that is headed to the United States.

Solution
Max gets a pen pal from the United States.

▲ On a separate sheet of paper, summarize the selection. Use the graphic organizer to help you. **Answers will vary.**

Practice Book
© Harcourt • Grade 3

Name _____

▲ Write a definition for each underlined word. Next to the definition, describe the context clues that helped you understand what the word means.

1. Lenny made three attempts to climb the rope before he finally did it.

   Tries; he tried to climb the rope three times before finally

   climbing it

2. Mr. Robert's red face and loud voice showed that he was furious.

   Very angry; a red face and loud voice usually are signs

   that someone is very angry

3. The fragile flowers could not live through cold weather.

   Delicate; because the flowers could not live through cold

   weather, they are not strong.

4. When Angela lost the contest, she was upset and felt dejected.

   Unhappy; if Angela lost, she would be upset and sad

5. Some animals hibernate, or rest and sleep, from late fall

   to early spring.

   Rest and sleep; the definition "rest and sleep" follows

   the word hibernate

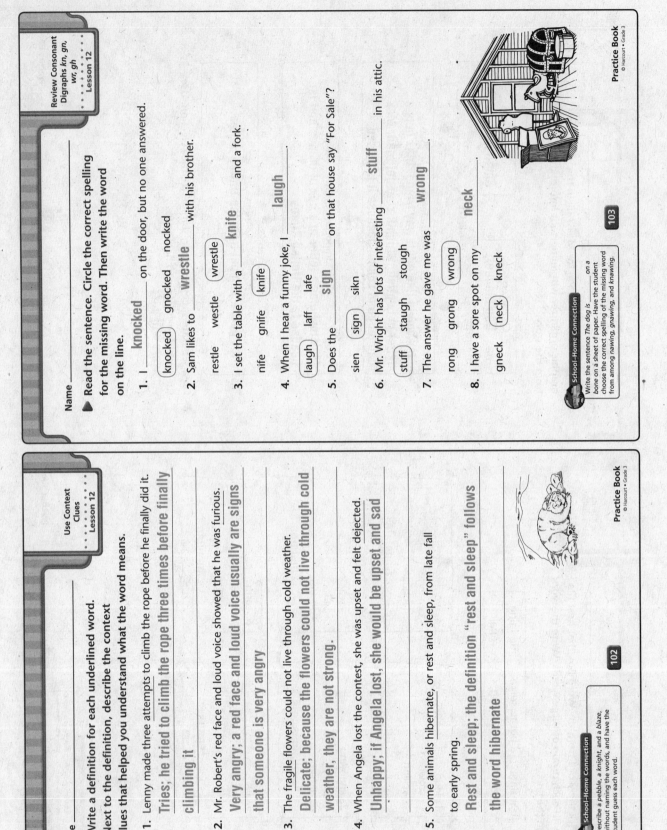

School–Home Connection
Describe a *pebble*, a *knight*, and a *blaze*, without naming the words, and have the student guess each word.

Practice Book
© Harcourt • Grade 3

Name _____

▲ Read the sentence. Circle the correct spelling for the missing word. Then write the word on the line.

1. I _knocked_ on the door, but no one answered.

   (knocked)   gnocked   nocked

2. Sam likes to _wrestle_ with his brother.

   restle   westle   (wrestle)

3. I set the table with a _knife_ and a fork.

   nife   gnife   (knife)

4. When I hear a funny joke, I _laugh_ _____.

   (laugh)   laff   lafe

5. Does the _sign_ on that house say "For Sale"?

   sien   (sign)   sikn

6. Mr. Wright has lots of interesting _stuff_ in his attic.

   (stuff)   staugh   stough

7. The answer he gave me was _wrong_ _____.

   rong   grong   (wrong)

8. I have a sore spot on my _neck_ _____.

   gneck   (neck)   kneck

School–Home Connection
Write the sentence *The dog is on a bone* on a sheet of paper. Have the student choose the correct spelling of the missing word from among *nawing, gnawing,* and *knawing.*

Practice Book
© Harcourt • Grade 3

© Harcourt • Grade 3

Student Edition pp. 102–103

Consonants /s/c, /j/g, dge
Lesson 13

Spelling Words
1. ice
2. age
3. rice
4. edge
5. stage
6. giant
7. range
8. judge
9. ledge
10. police
11. recent
12. bridge
13. office
14. strange
15. central

Name _____

▲ Read the Spelling Words. Sort the words and write them where they belong.

Words with /s/ Sound Spelled with c

1. ice
2. rice
3. police
4. recent
5. office
6. central

Words with /j/ Sound Spelled with g, or dge

7. age
8. edge
9. stage
10. giant
11. range
12. judge
13. ledge
14. bridge
15. strange

School-Home Connection
Help your child write a list of words that have the soft c or g sound. Discuss the correct spelling for each word. Together, confirm each spelling using a print or an online dictionary.

Practice Book
© Harcourt • Grade 3

105

Singular and Plural Pronouns
Lesson 12

Name _____

▲ Write the pronoun in each sentence. Then label each as *S* (singular) or *P* (plural).

1. We learned about Chile today. **We; P**
2. Mr. Edwards showed us two maps. **us; P**
3. He hung the maps on the wall. **He; S**
4. They showed volcanoes and a desert. **They; P**
5. The students looked at them carefully. **them; P**
6. Mr. Edwards asked me to point to the desert. **me; S**

▲ Rewrite each sentence with a correct pronoun. **Possible responses are shown.**

7. Ellen studied Spanish because _____ wanted to visit Spain.
   Ellen studied Spanish because she wanted to visit Spain.
8. The class was fun, and the students enjoyed _____.
   The class was fun, and the students enjoyed it.
9. The teacher brought pictures to show _____.
   The teacher brought pictures to shown them.
10. He took the pictures when _____ was in Spain.
    He took the pictures when he was in Spain.

School-Home Connection
Ask your child to write four sentences with pronouns. Then help him or her label each as S (singular) or P (plural).

Practice Book
© Harcourt • Grade 3

104

▲ Read each paragraph. Then write the answers to the questions.

A. Sam turned on his flashlight, and the thin beam of light cut through the darkness. The room was filled with old furniture. Dust and cobwebs covered everything. No one had been in this room for years. So what had made that strange moaning noise? He just *had* to find out!

B. Litterbugs are really becoming a problem in our neighborhood. The next time you are walking or biking around, take a look. Soda cans and candy wrappers are lying in the grass or floating on the pond. Nature is too beautiful for us to ruin it with trash. So do your part. Don't litter!

C. Milk has things the body needs. It has calcium to make your bones strong and help them grow. Calcium helps your teeth grow and stay healthy, too. Milk has lots of protein to build strong muscles.

1. What is the author's purpose in paragraph A? Who is the main character? The author's purpose is to entertain.

The main character is Sam.

2. What is the author's purpose in paragraph B? Why do you think so? The author's purpose is to persuade. The author is trying

to get readers to stop littering and writes, "Don't litter!"

3. What is the author's purpose in paragraph C? Why do you think so? The author's purpose is to inform or to teach. The author is

telling readers the good things that milk does for the body.

School-Home Connection
Have the student write three sentences to persuade you to do an activity with him or her. Remind the student to support the main idea with detail in the sentences.

106

Practice Book
© Harcourt • Grade 3

▲ Read the story. Complete the spelling of each word. Use -ge or -dge.

Last month, I was in a play called "The Lar __ge__ Bird."
The play takes place in a town called Bri __dge__ View. In the
story, a stran __ge__ oran __ge__ bird flies into town and
sits on a le __dge__ at the top of the town hall. The people of
the town try to capture the bird and put it in a ca __ge__ .
But they cannot quite reach the e __dge__ of the roof where
the bird is sitting!

I played a girl who is eight years of a __ge__ . She tells the
people that the bird is never going to bu __dge__ and that
they should just leave the bird alone. The people of the
town chan __ge__ their minds. They decide to let the bird
stay on top of the building. It is a great play!

School-Home Connection
Have the student tell a new story that uses several -ge and -dge words.

107

Practice Book
© Harcourt • Grade 3

Name _____

▲ **Part A.** Read each group of words. Write the Vocabulary Word that belongs in the group.

| dissolve | absorb | protects |
| rustling | columns | particles |

1. shields   guards   saves   **protects**

2. crackling   shuffling   crunching   **rustling**

3. melt   disappear   mix   **dissolve**

4. take in   soak up   sop up   **absorb**

▲ **Part B.** Complete the sentences. Possible responses are shown.

5. The **columns** of a library might be made out of _marble, stone,_ _concrete, or wood._

6. If you find **particles** of glass on your kitchen floor, someone probably _broke something made of glass._

7. To **protect** your CD collection, you should _keep it locked up_ _and keep the CDs clean._

8. Something that **dissolves** quickly in water is _sugar, salt, or_ _drink mix._

Name _____

▲ As you read "A Tree Is Growing," fill the graphic organizer. Possible responses are shown.

Section 1   pages 372-379

What I Know: Trees are living things.

What I Read: Even the biggest tree keeps growing and changing.

Author's Purpose Buds unfold into leaves.

Section 2   pages 380-387

What I Know: Trees grow slowly.

What I Read: Bristlecone pines are the oldest known living trees on earth.

Author's Purpose Trees can grow for thousands of years.

Section 3   pages 388-393

What I Know: Trees have leaves, bark, a trunk, and roots.

What I Read: Banyan tree roots grow down from the branches.

Author's Purpose Not all roots grow from the bottom of the tree's trunk.

1. What do you already know about trees?
   Trees have leaves, bark, a trunk, and roots.

2. What is the first thing you read about trees?
   Even the biggest tree keeps growing and changing.

▲ On a separate sheet of paper, summarize what you learned about trees. Use the graphic organizer to help you. Answers will vary.

Words with Consonants /s/c and /j/g dge — Lesson 13

▲ Each line of letters has two hidden words in which *c* is pronounced with the *s* sound or *g* is pronounced with the *j* sound. Circle the hidden words. Then write a sentence of your own that has both hidden words. **Possible responses are shown.**

1. c e j u o r a n (f o r c e) b l g e s p (g i a n t) c e c i o l

   You cannot force a giant to do something he does not

   want to do.

2. a c i f c e g i p (p e n c i l) g e r y (g e r m s) c e r w o t

   That pencil might have germs on it.

3. g (j u d g e) f g e n t l e v c e h t c i z t c i e g i d g

   The judge is a very gentle person.

4. o s k e r g e c i c (d a n c e) o l g i c e o l i m (s t a g e)

   I like to dance on stage.

5. g e a r c e i d g e c i e d g e (p r i n c e) t r a i p g i c

   The prince sat on the edge of the throne.

School–Home Connection
Have the student write a sentence that includes any two of the following words: *manager, celery, image,* or *circle.* Then invite him or her to read the sentence aloud.

Use Graphic Aids — Lesson 13

▲ Use the graphic aid to answer the questions. Circle the letter of the best answer to each question.

light
sun
carbon dioxide
oxygen
plant
soil
people and animals
water and minerals

1. What does the sun bring to the plant?

   A carbon dioxide
   B oxygen
   C water and minerals
   (D) light

2. What do people and animals bring to the plant?

   (A) carbon dioxide
   B oxygen
   C water and minerals
   D soil

3. What does the plant bring to people and animals?

   A carbon dioxide
   (B) oxygen
   C water and minerals
   D sun

School–Home Connection
Work with the student to create a graphic aid illustrating a system or process such as a weather pattern or how a flower grows.

Name _____

▲ Write a subject or object pronoun to replace each underlined word or phrase.

1. Ariel's sister taught Ariel about bees. __her__

2. Ariel's sister told Ariel that bees are insects. __She__

3. Ariel and I watched bees in the park. __We__

4. Ariel and I saw the bees fly. __them__

5. Ariel's father gave Ariel and me a book. __us__

6. The book had pictures of bees. __It__

▲ Rewrite each sentence. Use I and me correctly.

7. You and me picked pears from the tree.
   __You and I picked pears from the tree.__

8. Todd ate cherries with my friend and I.
   __Todd ate cherries with my friend and me.__

9. Me and my brother sliced apples.
   __My brother and I sliced apples.__

10. They shared the plums with me and him.
    __They shared the plums with him and me.__

School-Home Connection

Have your child write sentences using one or more of the following pronouns:
I you he she him her we they us

Practice Book
© Harcourt • Grade 3

© Harcourt • Grade 3

Spelling Words

1. robin
2. petal
3. seven
4. solid
5. final
6. given
7. color
8. hotel
9. wagon
10. music
11. total
12. cabin
13. taken
14. pupil
15. broken

Name _____

▲ Read the Spelling Words. Sort the words and write them where they belong.

Words that end with n

1. robin
2. seven
3. given
4. wagon
5. cabin
6. taken
7. broken

Words that end with l

8. petal
9. final
10. hotel
11. total
12. pupil

▲ Put the words that are left in alphabetical order.

13. color
14. music
15. solid

School-Home Connection

As you and your child discuss your daily activities, write down words that have the same syllable patterns as *robin* and *hotel*. Go over the list and have your child say and spell each word.

Practice Book
© Harcourt • Grade 3

V/CV and VC/V Syllable Patterns
Lesson 14

▲ Look at each pair of spelling words. Choose the word in each pair that has the V/CV syllable pattern, and write it on the lines. Use the boxed letters to answer the riddle at the bottom of the page.

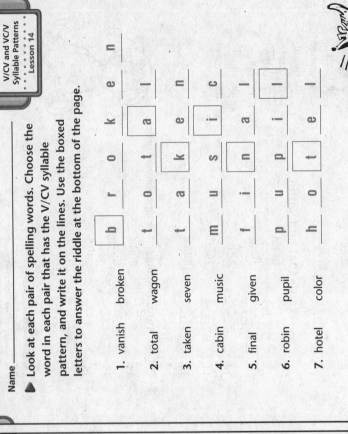

1. vanish   broken   b [r] o k e n

2. total   wagon   t o t [a] l

3. taken   seven   t [a] [k] e n

4. cabin   music   m u s [i] c

5. final   given   f [i] n a l

6. robin   pupil   p u p [i] l

7. hotel   color   h o [t] e l

Riddle:

Where can you leave your dog when you go to the mall?

Answer:

In the B   A   R   K   I   N   G   L   O   T
        1   2   3   4   5   6   7

School-Home Connection
Read the spelling words on the page to the student. Ask him or her to tell whether each word has a long or short vowel sound.

Author's Purpose
Lesson 14

▲ Read the selection. Then answer the questions that follow.

Leave the Logs Alone

Have you ever walked through a forest? If so, you probably have seen logs on the forest floor. Some people think these fallen trees are no longer useful. They think the logs should be removed to clean up the forest. But that's not true. Fallen trees still have a purpose.

Animals use these logs for shelter and to find food. If you gently rolled a log and peeked underneath, you would be surprised at what you would find. Worms, grubs, insects, and snakes make their homes in the cool mud beneath the logs. Removing the logs would mean that all of these creatures would have to find new homes.

In time, the logs will rot and become soil. New plants and trees will grow in that soil. This is another reason that fallen trees are important. As you can see, it is helpful to the forest to leave fallen trees where they are. We should leave the logs alone.

1. What was the author's purpose for writing this selection?

   to persuade

2. How does the title help you know this?

   "Leave the Logs Alone" tells people what to do.

3. What other sentences give you clues about the author's purpose?

   Possible response: As you can see, it is helpful to the

   forest to leave fallen trees where they are.

School-Home Connection
Have the student share a story with you. Work together to determine the author's purpose.

Name _____

Robust Vocabulary
Lesson 14

▲ **Part A.** Write the Vocabulary Word from the Word Box that matches each idea.

| maze | glimpse | spears |
| suppose | strikes | roost |

1. __suppose__ — when you think something may happen

2. __maze__ — a winding path that is like a puzzle

3. __roost__ — what a bird does to settle in a tree's branches

4. __glimpse__ — a quick peek at something

5. __strikes__ — when something hits someone

6. __spears__ — to stick a sharp object through something

▲ **Part B.** Use what you know about the Vocabulary Words in dark type to answer each question. Circle the answer within the sentence.

7. If you get a glimpse of a frog, do you get a long look or a (quick look)?

8. If someone spears a piece of fruit, does he (use a fork) or a spoon?

9. If a bird roosts, is it flying or (resting)?

10. If you are in a maze, are you on a straight path or a (winding path)?

11. If you suppose something, (might it happen) or did it happen already?

12. If something strikes you, does it (hit) you or hug you?

School-Home Connection
Ask the student what he or she supposes will happen tomorrow in school. Discuss whether this is something that has happened before or if it is something completely new.

Reader's Guide
Lesson 14

Name _____

▲ As you read "One Small Place in a Tree," fill in the first column of the graphic organizer with what you already know. In the middle column, write the information you read. Fill in the author's purpose after you finish the selection.

What I Know	What I Read	Author's Purpose

1. What is the main reason the author wrote the selection?
   __to tell about the ways animals use living and dead trees__

2. What is the author's purpose?
   __to inform__

▲ On a separate sheet of paper, summarize the selection. Use the graphic organizer to help you. **Answers will vary.**

Name _____

▲ The following graph shows the kinds of trees in Sunshine Park. Use the information in the graph to answer the questions. Answer each question with a complete sentence.

Trees in Sunshine Park

1. What kinds of trees does Sunshine Park have?
   The park has oak, pine, maple, fir, and birch trees.

2. How many maple trees are there in the park?
   There are eight maple trees in the park.

3. What kind of tree has the fewest number in the park?
   Fir trees have the fewest number in the park.

4. How many pine trees are there in the park?
   There are three pine trees in the park.

5. The park has an equal number of which two kinds of trees?
   The park has an equal number of pine and birch.

School-Home Connection
Work with the student to create a new graph using the following information: ash trees, 10; cherry trees, 7; willow trees, 2.

© Harcourt • Grade 3

Practice Book
© Harcourt • Grade 3

Name _____

▲ Use these VCV words to complete each sentence. Then circle those words in the puzzle. Look for them across and down.

| cozy | baby | total | habit | tulips |
| pupils | future | visits | seven | equal |

1. There are six or ___**seven**___ ___**pupils**___ in the classroom.

2. The ___**baby**___ will be an adult in the ___**future**___.

3. When Ari ___**visits**___, he has a ___**habit**___ of always being late.

4. The ___**total**___ number of items on a balanced scale is ___**equal**___ on each side.

5. The bunny looked ___**cozy**___ sleeping in the bed of colorful ___**tulips**___.

School-Home Connection
Ask the student to tell where each VCV word is divided into syllables. Then have him or her suggest other VCV words that could be used to complete the sentences.

Practice Book
© Harcourt • Grade 3

Name _____

▲ Circle the pronoun in each sentence. Rewrite the sentence. Correct the pronoun so that it agrees with the underlined word.

1. The nest was too high for Maria to see (him).
   The nest was too high for Maria to see it.

2. Maria was excited because (he) saw an owl.
   Maria was excited because she saw an owl.

3. Luke was homesick when (it) went to camp.
   Luke was homesick when he went to camp.

4. The girls invited Hillary to play with (her).
   The girls invited Hillary to play with them.

5. John wrote a letter and sent (them) home.
   John wrote a letter and sent it home.

6. John's parents wrote back to (it).
   John's parents wrote back to him.

▲ Fill in each blank with a correct pronoun. Then underline the word or words that the pronoun refers to.

7. Honeybees live in hives, where __they__ have jobs to do.

8. Worker bees feed the queen bee and protect __her__ .

9. Honeybees gather nectar and use __it__ to make honey.

10. Some people keep bees and collect honey from __them__ .

School-Home Connection
Ask your child to write three sentences about family members, using their names. Then ask him or her to rewrite the sentences, replacing the names with pronouns.

Name _____

▲ Read the -le words in the Word Box. Write each word on a line below. Then divide each word into syllables.

table	cable	title
maple	noble	staple

C-le Words

ta l ble

ca l ble

ti l tle

ma l ple

sta l ple

sta l ple

Write two more C-le syllable pattern words.
Possible response: cradle, uncle

Choose a C-le word from the Word Box. Write a sentence using that word.
Possible response: The leaves of the maple tree turn yellow and orange in the autumn.

School-Home Connection
Have the student think of other -le words. Discuss how to divide the new words into syllables.

Name _____

▲ Fold the paper along the dotted line. As each spelling word is read aloud, write it on the line. Then unfold the paper and check your work.

Spelling Words
1. title
2. rattle
3. saddle
4. gnat
5. knight
6. wrench
7. rough
8. edge
9. police
10. giant
11. judge
12. hotel
13. seven
14. broken
15. taken

1. _____
2. _____
3. _____
4. _____
5. _____
6. _____
7. _____
8. _____
9. _____
10. _____
11. _____
12. _____
13. _____
14. _____
15. _____

School-Home Connection
Ask the student to write five sentences using his or her favorite spelling words from the list above.

122

Practice Book
© Harcourt • Grade 3

Name _____

▲ Circle the words in each sentence that contain kn, gn, wr, or gh. Then, write the words in the crossword puzzle.

1. There is a wrinkle in my new shirt.
2. I tapped on the door with my knuckles.
3. The knight rode a white horse.
4. We knew all the answers on the spelling test.
5. She put wrapping paper on the gift for her friend.
6. He had a bad cough while he was sick.
7. Can you hear the laughter on the playground?
8. Turn left at the stop sign.

Crossword: 1. wrinkle 2. knight 3. knight 4. knew 5. wrapping 6. cough 7. laughter 8. sign

School-Home Connection
Ask the student to think of other words that contain kn, gn, wr, and gh. Help him or her add several of these words to the puzzle.

123

Practice Book
© Harcourt • Grade 3

Name _____

▲ **Read the story. Then answer the questions.**

Sumi could not believe that today had finally arrived! She had waited all summer for her birthday. She and her mom had planned for weeks. They called it "The Big Beach Birthday Bash." She had invited all her friends for games, swimming, and a cookout at the beach.

Sumi's excitement quickly ended when she looked out the window. Dark storm clouds filled the sky. Within minutes, lightning cracked and rain poured down. She had never been so disappointed.

"We'll figure something out," her mom assured her.

Meanwhile, Sumi's dad took her to the grocery store to pick up meat for the burgers and ice for the cooler.

"Why are we buying this?" she asked. "We can't go to the beach in the rain."

When they got back home, Sumi opened the door.

"Surprise!" her friends shouted.

There were plastic swimming pools full of sand in the living room for sand-castle contests. There were beach chairs and picnic blankets all around the house. Her dad's grill was on the back porch. Sumi would have her party after all!

1. Who are the characters? Sumi, her parents, her friends

2. What is the setting? Sumi's house, the grocery store

3. What is the problem? Sumi could not have her party at the beach because of the rain.

4. What is the solution? Sumi's mom made their house look like the beach and moved the party indoors.

School-Home Connection

Have the student tell you a story about a party. Remind him or her to include all of the elements of plot including a problem and a beginning, middle, and ending.

124   Practice Book
© Harcourt • Grade 3

Name _____

▲ **Read this part of a student's rough draft. Then answer the questions that follow.**

(1) Tony is the friend of Joan. (2) Tony tells Joan that he is upset. (3) Joan asks he what is wrong. (4) Tony says that he lost his mothers pen. (5) Joan helps him look for the pen. (6) Together they find it under Tony's bed.

1. Which sentence has a singular possessive noun?
   A Sentence 2
   B Sentence 3
   C Sentence 5
   D Sentence 6

2. Which sentence has an incorrectly written possessive noun?
   A Sentence 2
   B Sentence 3
   C Sentence 4
   D Sentence 6

3. Which phrase could replace the underlined phrase in Sentence 1?
   A the friend's of Joan
   B the friends of Joan
   C Joan's friend
   D Joans' friend

4. Which pronoun could replace the underlined word in Sentence 2?
   A he
   B she
   C him
   D her

5. Which pronoun could replace the underlined phrase in Sentence 5?
   A it
   B her
   C him
   D them

6. Which sentence has an incorrect pronoun?
   A Sentence 3
   B Sentence 4
   C Sentence 5
   D Sentence 6

Name _____

▲ Follow the path from the arrow to the finish line. Shade only the boxes that have a word with the soft c or soft g sound. Then answer the questions.

Start	stage	forget	coat	uncover	popcorn	gum
guppy	edge	celery	castle	mice	margin	trace
stag	game	engine	pack	prince	tic	finish
cast	green	cell	voice	judge	gave	leg

1. Which words in the puzzle end with -dge? **edge, judge**

2. Which words end with the letters -ice? **voice, mice**

3. Which word ends with the letters -ace? **trace**

4. Write three words from above that have the soft c sound. Possible response: **celery, cell, prince**

5. Write three words from above that have the soft g sound. Possible response: **stage, margin, engine**

School-Home Connection
With the student, make up a silly sentence that includes as many words with the soft c sound as possible. Repeat by making up a sentence with soft g words.

126   Practice Book
© Harcourt • Grade 3

Name _____

▲ Part A. Write the meaning of each word in dark type. Underline the clues that helped you figure out the meaning of that word.

1. Mom asked me to put the forks in the drawer with the other **utensils**.

   Utensils means _tools to eat with, such as forks._

2. Mario's new glasses **magnify** things, making them bigger and easier for him to see.

   Magnify means _to make bigger and easier to see._

3. The President is elected by the **citizens** that live in our country.

   Citizens means _people living in our country._

4. All the noise and confusion was quite a **commotion**.

   Commotion means _noise and confusion._

5. The collector said it was hard to find **obscure** artwork that not many people knew about.

   Obscure means _hard to find and not well known._

▲ Part B. Fill in the blanks, using some words in dark type from above.

6. We set the table with plates, cups, and _utensils_.

7. Patti had to _magnify_ the tiny print to be able to see it.

8. All of the _commotion_ at the playground made it hard to sit and read.

School-Home Connection
With the student, look for other unfamiliar words and use context clues to determine their meaning.

127   Practice Book
© Harcourt • Grade 3

Name _____

▲ **Part A.** Use the meaning of the underlined Vocabulary Word to complete each sentence. **Possible responses are shown.**

1. I would need to ask for advice if __I had an important decision__ __to make and did not know what to do.__

2. If a friend asked me to recommend something fun to do on a rainy day, I would suggest __reading a good book__ because __I love to listen to the sound of the rain while I read.__

3. It would not be sensible to __cross the street without looking__ __both ways first.__

4. I always consult __my parents__ when __I want to invite a friend to spend the night.__

▲ **Part B.** Write a sentence for the Vocabulary Words *issue* and *devise.*

Possible response: Ruth enjoyed reading the new issue of

her favorite magazine. _____

Possible response: Together we can devise a plan to keep

opossums safe from traffic. _____

_____

School-Home Connection
With the student, think of a time when you have offered advice. Discuss the situation, challenging the student to use as many of the Vocabulary Words as possible.

Name _____

▲ There are five V/CV words and five VC/V words in the puzzle. The V/CV words are written down. The VC/V words are written across. Circle the words in the puzzle. Then write each one in the correct box at the bottom of the page.

a	t	i	g	e	r	k	s
r	b	a	c	o	r	n	o
i	t	o	t	a	l	v	l
v	w	h	r	s	t	e	i
e	a	e	q	i	r	d	d
r	g	b	n	y	p	y	t
a	o	i	p	u	p	i	l
z	n	t	m	e	v	e	n

V/CV	VC/V
tiger	river
acorn	wagon
total	habit
pupil	very
even	solid

School-Home Connection
Have the student think of three other V/CV and three other VC/V words. Then work together to make a word-search puzzle that includes these words.

Name _____

▲ Read the article. On the lines below it, write your answers to the questions about the author's purpose.

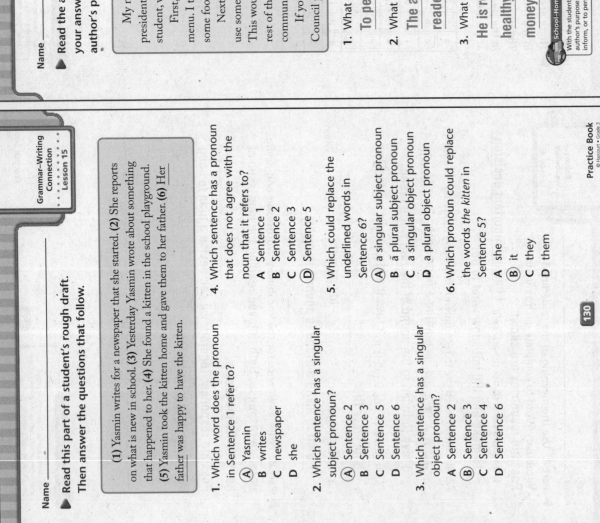

My name is William Wu. I would like to be your Student Council president. I think I would make a good president. I am a responsible student, with exciting ideas for improving our school.

First, I would work with the school to change the school lunch menu. I think it should include some healthy choices. It should also have some foods everyone likes.

Next, I would like our school to have a carnival every year. We could use some of the money we make to buy a new computer for the library. This would help all of our students. We could give the rest of the money to a good cause. This would help our community.

If you like these ideas, vote for me for Student Council president.

1. What was the author's purpose for writing the article?

   To persuade

2. What clues helped you figure out the author's purpose?

   The author wants people to vote for him. He tries to make

   readers think that that he would be a good president.

3. What does William want readers to know?

   He is responsible, he will improve the lunch menu by offering

   healthy choices, and he would like to have a carnival to raise

   money for a new computer and to donate to charity.

School-Home Connection

With the student, create a story. Decide on the author's purpose. Will it be to entertain, to inform, or to persuade?

Name _____

▲ Read this part of a student's rough draft. Then answer the questions that follow.

(1) Yasmin writes for a newspaper that she started. (2) She reports on what is new in school. (3) Yesterday Yasmin wrote about something that happened to her. (4) She found a kitten in the school playground. (5) Yasmin took the kitten home and gave them to her father. (6) Her father was happy to have the kitten.

1. Which word does the pronoun in Sentence 1 refer to?
   Ⓐ Yasmin
   B writes
   C newspaper
   D she

2. Which sentence has a singular subject pronoun?
   Ⓐ Sentence 2
   B Sentence 3
   C Sentence 5
   D Sentence 6

3. Which sentence has a singular object pronoun?
   A Sentence 2
   Ⓑ Sentence 3
   C Sentence 4
   D Sentence 6

4. Which sentence has a pronoun that does not agree with the noun that it refers to?
   A Sentence 1
   B Sentence 2
   C Sentence 3
   Ⓓ Sentence 5

5. Which could replace the underlined words in Sentence 6?
   Ⓐ a singular subject pronoun
   B a plural subject pronoun
   C a singular object pronoun
   D a plural object pronoun

6. Which pronoun could replace the words the kitten in Sentence 5?
   A she
   Ⓑ it
   C they
   D them

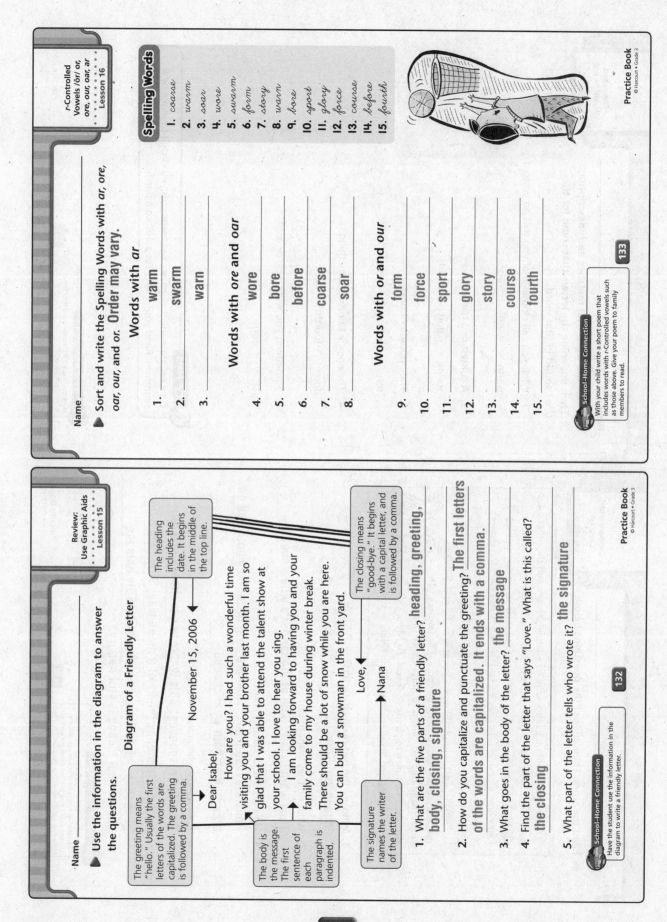

© Harcourt • Grade 3

Name _____

▲ Use the information in the diagram to answer the questions.

Diagram of a Friendly Letter

The heading includes the date. It begins in the middle of the top line.

November 15, 2006

Dear Isabel,

The greeting means "hello." Usually the first letters of the words are capitalized. The greeting is followed by a comma.

How are you? I had such a wonderful time visiting you and your brother last month. I am so glad that I was able to attend the talent show at your school. I love to hear you sing.

I am looking forward to having you and your family come to my house during winter break. There should be a lot of snow while you are here. You can build a snowman in the front yard.

The body is the message. The first sentence of each paragraph is indented.

Love,

Nana

The signature names the writer of the letter.

The closing means "good-bye." It begins with a capital letter, and is followed by a comma.

1. What are the five parts of a friendly letter? **heading, greeting, body, closing, signature**

2. How do you capitalize and punctuate the greeting? **The first letters of the words are capitalized. It ends with a comma.**

3. What goes in the body of the letter? **the message**

4. Find the part of the letter that says "Love." What is this called? **the closing**

5. What part of the letter tells who wrote it? **the signature**

Practice Book
© Harcourt • Grade 3

School-Home Connection
Have the student use the information in the diagram to write a friendly letter.

Name _____

r-Controlled
Vowels /ôr/ or,
ore, our, oar, ar
Lesson 16

▲ Sort and write the Spelling Words with *ar, ore, oar, our,* and *or*. **Order may vary.**

Spelling Words

1. coarse
2. warm
3. soar
4. wore
5. swarm
6. form
7. story
8. warn
9. bore
10. sport
11. glory
12. force
13. course
14. before
15. fourth

Words with *ar*

1. warm
2. swarm
3. warn

Words with *ore* and *oar*

4. wore
5. bore
6. before
7. coarse
8. soar

Words with *or* and *our*

9. form
10. force
11. sport
12. glory
13. story
14. course
15. fourth

Practice Book
© Harcourt • Grade 3

School-Home Connection
With your child write a short poem that includes words with r-Controlled vowels such as those above. Give your poem to family members to read.

69

Student Edition pp. 132–133

Name _____

▲ Circle the word that matches each description.
Then underline the letters that stand for the
/ôr/ sound in that word.

1. What you call clothes that you had on yesterday

   warm   [worn]   worse

2. A contest or a game

   spring   [sport]   splash

3. The opposite of *after*

   fort   because   [before]

4. The energy to move something

   [force]   fourth   farce

5. Something you write, tell, or read

   [story]   sorry   stare

Try This

On a separate sheet of paper, use the words you circled to make new
sentences. Read your sentences aloud to a partner.

School-Home Connection
Have the student tell a story using the circled
words from above.

	135

Name _____

▲ Read the story. Then answer the questions below.

Two mice lived on a farm. One was named Meany, and the other
was named Silly. One day the farmer's wife set a big piece of cheese on
the kitchen table. Both mice looked at it, and their stomachs rumbled. "I
know how we can get the cheese," said Meany. "I will scare the farmer's
wife so that she bumps into the table and knocks the cheese to the floor.
Then you will scare her so that she runs out the door."

Silly shook his head. "I know a better way," he said. Silly ran
into the kitchen and did a funny dance. The farmer's wife
laughed and laughed. She liked Silly's dance so much
that she gave him a big hunk of cheese. To Meany, she
gave nothing, and his stomach is still rumbling to this very day.

1. Who are the two main characters?
   Meany and Silly

2. What do they want to do?
   They want to get some of the farmer's wife's cheese.

3. How are the characters alike?
   Possible responses: They are both mice; they both live on
   a farm; they both want cheese.

4. How are the characters different?
   Possible responses: Silly wants to get cheese in a fun
   way, while Meany thinks of a mean way; Silly gets a hunk
   of cheese, while Meany gets nothing; Silly eats the
   cheese, but Meany is still hungry.

School-Home Connection
Help the student compare and contrast two
characters in a story he or she enjoys. Ask the
student to tell how the characters are alike and
how they are different.

	134

Name _____

▲ **Part A**

Write the Vocabulary Word from the box below that completes each sentence.

| disguised | cunning | embraced |
| tender | brittle | delighted |

1. When you use a costume to hide who you are, you are __disguised__

2. If something is __brittle__, it may break apart if you squeeze it.

3. A __cunning__ person can play a clever trick on you.

4. If you can cut something easily, it is probably __tender__.

5. When people win a prize, they feel __delighted__.

6. Ruth __embraced__ her grandmother when she arrived for a visit.

▲ **Part B**

Write a sentence to answer each question.

7. What could a child do to delight his or her mother? **Possible response: The child could sing a song to his mother.**

8. How would you know if a friend was disguised? **Possible response: She would look different from what she usually looks like. She may be wearing a mask.**

School-Home Connection

Help the student name synonyms for the following Vocabulary Words: *tender, delighted,* and *cunning.* Then have him or her choose one word and use it in a written sentence.

Name _____

▲ As you read "Lon Po Po," fill in the graphic organizer with details about how the characters are alike and different. Then answer the questions.

Shang — Both — Wolf

1. How is Shang different from the wolf? **Possible response: Shang is the eldest of the three children.**

2. How are Shang and the wolf alike? **Possible response: They both live in China. They both want to eat gingko nuts.**

▲ On a separate sheet of paper, summarize the selection. Use the graphic organizer to help you.

Name _____

▲ **For each rhyme, underline the word with the prefix or suffix. Then write the prefix or suffix in the correct column.**

	Prefix	Suffix
		ful

1. Thomas was a cheerful lad.
   He laughed a lot and was never sad.

| | | less |

2. Sam was sleepless every night.
   His brother would not turn off the light.

| | re | |

3. I read a story I liked quite well.
   If you want to hear it, I will retell.

| | un | |

4. Don't be unhappy. Please don't cry.
   I know you can do it, if you try.

| | | ful |

5. A dog is a wonderful pet for you.
   Cats and birds make nice friends, too.

| | | ful |

6. Shonda was careful when riding her bike.
   She did not want to hit her buddy, Mike.

Name _____

r-Controlled
Vowels: or, ore,
our, ar, oar
Lesson 16

▲ **Read the story. Find ten words with the /ôr/ sound spelled or, ore, our, ar, or oar. Underline them. Then write the word and the letters that stand for the /ôr/ sound on the lines below.**

Will was on vacation with his family. It was their first day in Florida. Will was so excited that he jumped out of bed. He couldn't wait to see the Atlantic Ocean. But then he heard his sister, Cora, say, "It's pouring outside! Look, Will!"

"We won't be visiting the seashore today," he told her. "It looks like you can put away that surfboard."

"Of course, I warned you," said Cora. "The weather forecast said it would be stormy today. But you didn't listen to me."

Then the cordless telephone rang. It was their cousin, Jorge. He invited Will and Cora to his home to play card games!

1. Florida; or
2. Cora; or
3. pouring; our
4. seashore; ore
5. surfboard; oar
6. course; our
7. warned; ar
8. forecast; ore
9. stormy; or
10. cordless; or

72

Student Edition pp. 138–139

© Harcourt • Grade 3

Page 140 — Adjectives, Lesson 16

© Harcourt • Grade 3

Name _____

▲ Underline the two adjectives in each sentence. Then write whether each adjective tells *what kind* or *how many*.

1. Many wolves eat five pounds of food a day.

   how many; how many

2. A few wolves have blue eyes.

   how many; what kind

3. The coats of some wolves are white.

   how many; what kind

4. Big wolves weigh more than ninety pounds.

   what kind; how many

▲ Rewrite the sentences. Add an adjective before each underlined noun. Use an adjective that answers the question in parentheses ( ).
Possible responses are shown.

5. The apple fell from the tree. (What color?)

   The red apple fell from the tree.

6. There were apples on the tree. (How many?)

   There were many apples on the tree.

7. Fatima ate the apple. (What size?)

   Fatima ate the big apple.

8. I cut the apple into slices. (What shape?)

   I cut the round apple into slices.

School-Home Connection
Ask your child to make a list of things in your home. Help him or her think of an adjective to describe each noun. The adjectives should tell what kind or how many.

140 Practice Book
© Harcourt • Grade 3

Page 141 — r-Controlled Vowels /ûr/ er, ir, ur, or, ear, Lesson 17

Name _____

Spelling Words

1. word
2. girl
3. burn
4. work
5. hurt
6. verse
7. purse
8. clerk
9. earth
10. perfect
11. frost
12. pearl
13. answer
14. person
15. thirsty

▲ Read the Spelling Words. Write each word in the group where it belongs.

Words with *er*

1. verse
2. clerk
3. perfect
4. answer
5. person

Words with *ir*

6. girl
7. first
8. thirsty

Words with *ur*

9. burn
10. hurt
11. purse

Words with *or*

12. word
13. work

Words with *ear*

14. earth
15. pearl

School-Home Connection
Read labels on food containers or clothing with your child. Find words with the r- Controlled vowels (er, ir, ur, or, ear) and write them down. Discuss the spelling of these words.

141 Practice Book
© Harcourt • Grade 3

Student Edition pp. 140–141

r-Controlled Vowel: er, ir, and ur
Lesson 17

▲ In each sentence below, you will find a word with the /ûr/ sound. Circle that word and underline the letters that stand for the /ûr/ sound.

1. My baby cousin just got his [first] tooth.

2. The car [swerved] to miss the hole in the road.

3. Each [person] who came received a free book.

4. Sasha plays [third] base on our softball team.

5. Li's new [shirt] is black and red.

6. Ms. Sanchez gave the class a [stern] look.

7. I was careful not to [burn] myself on the hot stove.

8. That baseball card is [worth] much more than I paid for it.

9. A strange car [turned] into the driveway.

10. The panting dog was very [thirsty].

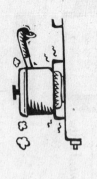

School-Home Connection
Have the student pronounce all the words with the underlined letter combinations er, ir, and ur. Then help him or her make up a story using those words.

Practice Book
© Harcourt • Grade 3

143

Compare and Contrast
Lesson 17

▲ Read the two story beginnings. Then write the answers to the questions.

Story Beginning 1

Lin stood in the kitchen waiting for her older brother, Aki. She turned on the light so she could see in the dark green kitchen. Then she opened the cabinet by the sink. Everything they needed was there. She pulled out yellow sponges, a bottle of liquid soap, washcloths, and a bottle of window cleaner. Aki came down the kitchen stairs with two buckets. Now, they were ready for a car wash.

Story Beginning 2

Angela watered the flowers on the kitchen table. Her sister, Georgette, put the clean dishes away. After Georgette was done, it was time for their checkers game. Every day after they cleaned up the kitchen, they played checkers on the kitchen table. Angela thought that the bright yellow kitchen kept her focused and alert.

1. How are the two main characters alike?
Both are girls; both have siblings; both are going to do an activity with a family member.

2. How are the two families different?
Lin has a brother, and Angela has a sister.

3. How are the two settings alike?
They are both kitchens.

4. How are the two settings different?
The first kitchen is dark green. The second kitchen is bright yellow.

School-Home Connection
Help the student compare and contrast two things that are in the room. Ask how these things are alike. How are they different?

142

Practice Book
© Harcourt • Grade 3

Robust Vocabulary
Lesson 17

Name _____

▲ **Part A.** Complete each sentence with one of the Vocabulary Words in the box.

scolding	console	drowsy
glancing	heroic	burden

1. Two heavy piles of clothes are a __burden__ to carry.

2. A sleepy child looks __drowsy__.

3. A person with courage can be __heroic__.

4. One reason for hugging people is to __console__ them when they are feeling bad.

5. When someone looks quickly around a room, he or she is __glancing__.

6. If I talk sternly to a child, I am probably __scolding__ him or her.

▲ **Part B.** Write an answer to each question.

7. Why would you be glancing around in a restaurant?
Possible response: to see if I know anyone there

8. Why might you feel drowsy?
Possible response: because I need sleep

School-Home Connection
Ask the student to talk about when a lifeguard might be *heroic*. Ask him or her to describe the heroic action.

Practice Book
© Harcourt • Grade 3

144

Reader's Guide
Lesson 17

Name _____

▲ As you read "Two Bear Cubs," fill in the graphic organizer with details about how Older Brother and Younger Brother are alike and different. Then answer the questions.

Older Brother   Both   Younger Brother

1. How is Older Brother different from Younger Brother?
Possible response: Older Brother wants to see what is downriver. Younger Brother wants to obey their mother.

2. How are Younger Brother and Older Brother alike?
Possible response: Both disobey their mother.

▲ On a separate sheet of paper, summarize the selection. Use the graphic organizer to help you.

Practice Book
© Harcourt • Grade 3

145

Left Page

Name _____

Prefixes and Suffixes
Lesson 17

▲ Form a word from each root word and each prefix or suffix. Then write a sentence for each word that you made. **Possible responses are shown.**

1. dis + agree
   My friends *disagree* about what movie to watch.

2. dis + appeared
   The dolphins *disappeared* from our sight.

3. long + er
   My hair is *longer* than my sister's.

4. soft + er
   Cotton is *softer* than sandpaper.

5. dark + est
   The *darkest* puppy had brown spots.

6. strong + est
   The *strongest* tree survived the windstorm.

7. quick + ly
   Students leave *quickly* after the bell rings.

School-Home Connection
Have the student pick two words with suffixes from above and help him or her write a sentence that uses both words.

146

Practice Book
© Harcourt • Grade 3

Right Page

Review Controlled Vowel:
er, ir, ur, or, ear
Lesson 17

Name _____

▲ Read each question. Circle the words in each question that have the letter combinations *er, ir, ur, ear,* and *or.* Then circle the word that answers that question.

1. Which animal has (fur) and (searches) for nuts?
   a spider   an alligator   (a squirrel)

2. Who (works) to help people feel healthy?
   an actor   (a nurse)   a tailor

3. What is less than (thirty-two?)
   (thirty-five)   (thirty-one)   (thirty-eight)

4. Which animal might live beneath a (fern) and crawl through the (dirt?)
   a blackbird   (an earthworm)   a tiger

5. Which (word) names a (person) who sails on the sea?
   learner   tractor   (sailor)

6. Which could help you (survive) a cold night outside in (early) (January?)
   doing a crossword puzzle   (burning wood)   watching birds

School-Home Connection
Have the student tell you how he or she knew which were the correct answers.

147

Practice Book
© Harcourt • Grade 3

© Harcourt • Grade 3

76

Student Edition pp. 146–147

Name _____

▲ Write the form of each adjective that compares two things. Then write the form that compares three or more things.

1. playful   __more playful__, __most playful__

2. funny   __funnier__, __funniest__

3. afraid   __more afraid__, __most afraid__

4. important   __more important__, __most important__

5. high   __higher__, __highest__

6. exciting   __more exciting__, __most exciting__

▲ Rewrite each sentence correctly.

7. The raccoon was small than the fox.
__The raccoon was smaller than the fox.__

8. Today's sunset was lovely than yesterday's sunset.
__Today's sunset was lovelier than yesterday's sunset.__

9. That cliff was the most steep one I have ever climbed.
__That cliff was the steepest one I have ever climbed.__

10. The river was more deeper than the stream.
__The river was deeper than the stream.__

Practice Book
© Harcourt • Grade 3

School-Home Connection
With your child, take turns writing sentences that compare things in your home. (Examples: *This plant is taller than that one. That is the biggest bowl in the house.*)

Name _____

▲ Write the Spelling Words on cards. Lay them down and read them.

1. Circle the base word in each Spelling Word.

2. If the Spelling Word has a base word that ends with a consonant, write it in the correct part of the chart.

3. If the Spelling Word has a base word that ends with a vowel, write it in the other part of the chart.

Spelling Words

1. nicer
2. finest
3. useful
4. bigger
5. really
6. nicest
7. faster
8. lonely
9. quickly
10. careful
11. smaller
12. playful
13. biggest
14. slowly
15. thankful

Base Words That End with a Consonant	Base Words That End with a Vowel
1. bigger	10. nicer
2. really	11. finest
3. faster	12. useful
4. quickly	13. nicest
5. smaller	14. lonely
6. playful	15. careful
7. biggest	
8. slowly	
9. thankful	

Practice Book
© Harcourt • Grade 3

School-Home Connection
Have your child retell a familiar short story as you write it down. Then have him or her circle all of the words that have the suffixes -er, -est, -ly, and -ful.

Student Edition pp. 148–149

▲ Read the story. Circle the words with the suffixes -er and -est. On the lines below, list those words and write their root words beside them.

Twila and Carlos walked along the beach. "Hey!" shouted Twila. "Look at this rock. It is the shiniest rock I have ever seen!"

Carlos held out his hand. "This rock is shinier," he said. "It is also bigger."

Twila frowned. "My rock is nicer than yours," she said. "It is pointier, too."

"I do not like pointy rocks," said Carlos. "I like round rocks. Mine is rounder than yours."

"Well," said Twila. "I do not like round rocks. I like red rocks. Mine is redder than yours."

"Mine is the reddest!" shouted Carlos.

"Children," called their mother. "Why are you both shouting? You are being the noisiest, silliest children I have ever seen."

1. shiniest, shiny

2. shinier, shiny

3. bigger, big

4. nicer, nice

5. pointier, pointy

6. rounder, round

7. redder, red

8. reddest, red

9. noisiest, noisy

10. silliest, silly

 School-Home Connection
Have the student make a list of five -er words and five -est words.

▲ Read the story. Circle the letter of the best answer to each question. Underline the clues in the story that helped you answer the first question.

Allie's Wheels

"I can't get this go-cart to work," Allie cried. She put down the wheel she had been trying to fit on the cart. "I'm tired of trying!" Her mother picked up the wheel. "It will be fine. You just have to keep at it."

"But it's ugly," Allie said. "And I can't fix it!" She ran out of the garage and into her bedroom.

That night, Allie could not sleep. She thought about her go-cart. Slowly, she began to think of ways to make it better. She figured out how to attach the wheels so they would not fall off. She decided to paint the go-cart so it would not look so plain. In the morning, she hurried to the garage. Before her mother was up, Allie was hard at work. When her mother came into the garage, she was surprised. "Wow, Allie, your go-cart looks amazing!" she exclaimed.

"And look," Allie said, driving it out of the garage. "I've got wheels!"

1. What is the theme of this story?
A It is easy to make a go-cart.
B Even if something is hard to do, keep trying and you may do it.
C Stop trying if something is difficult to do.
D Having wheels is amazing.

2. What is a clue that helped tell what the theme is?
A Allie could not sleep.
B Her mother picked up the wheel.
C Allie could not fix the go-cart.
D Allie was hard at work.

School-Home Connection
Have the student make up a story of his or her own with this same theme.

Name _____

▲ Use the Vocabulary Words from the box below to complete the sentences.

| glorious | memory | crept |
| ruined | streak | yanked |

1. If you are looking at something ___glorious___, then it must be very beautiful.

2. He ___yanked___ the rope, and pulled the basket out of the water.

3. The cat ___crept___ slowly across the grass as it watched the bird.

4. Our rocket ship was ___ruined___ when it landed on its side.

5. The plane left a lovely white ___streak___ when it flew over the mountain peak.

6. My favorite ___memory___ is of my kitten playing with yarn.

School-Home Connection

Help the student write a sentence of his or her own with one of the Vocabulary Words.

© Harcourt • Grade 3

Name _____

▲ As you read "Me and Uncle Romie," fill in the graphic organizer to understand the story structure and theme. Use the page numbers to find what goes in each box.

Section 1 pages 90, 91

Setting
New York City

Characters
James, Uncle Romie, Aunt Nanette

Section 2 pages 90, 98

Plot

Problem
James does not feel comfortable visiting his Uncle Romie. Aunt Nanette leaves James alone with Uncle Romie. James thinks his birthday is ruined.

Section 3 pages 91, 93, 94, 98, 99, 101, 103, 104, 105, 106

Events
James comes to New York City. James learns about Uncle Romie's art. Uncle Romie helps James celebrate his birthday at a baseball game. James goes to Uncle Romie's art show. Uncle Romie gives James a special collage. James makes a special collage for Uncle Romie.

Section 4 pages 100, 103

Solution
Uncle Romie shared his art with James and celebrated his birthday at a baseball game.

Theme
Art can use memories to help bring families together.

▲ These directions tell how to make a paper airplane. Add a time-order word from the box to each step. Write the word on the line.

second	first	next	third	finally

How to Make a Paper Airplane

1. **First** _____, take a piece of paper.

2. **Second** _____, fold down one end of the paper to meet the middle. Do the same with the other end. You will have a sharp point at one end of the paper.

3. **Third** _____, fold down the remaining sides of the paper. You will have an even sharper point at the same end.

4. **Next** _____, fold the edges back over so that the slanted edges are together.

5. **Finally** _____, you are ready to fly your plane. Turn it over, place your fingers on the bottom edge, and let it glide through the air.

School-Home Connection Have the student retell the directions for making a paper airplane in his or her own words. Encourage the student to use time-order words.

▲ Read the story. Find the words with incorrect suffixes. Cross out those words. Then choose the correctly spelled words from the Word Box below, and write them above the words you crossed out.

carefully	sternly	loudly	happiest	worriedly
playful	respectful	joyfully	higher	beautiful

beautiful

It was a ~~beautier~~ day. The Outdoor Club members hiked up the

higher

mountain. Viya was the ~~happier~~ of all. She was going to hike ~~highest~~

happiest
carefully

than she had ever hiked before. She hiked ~~carefullest~~, though. She did

not want to fall.

worriedly

Suddenly, Sven gave a shout. "I see a bear," he cried ~~worriedful~~.

loudly

"Everyone start singing ~~loudful~~," said Ms. Packer. "That will scare

the bear away."

joyfully

"Look," called Viya ~~joyfulest~~. "The bear has two cubs. Oh, they are

playful

so ~~playly~~!"

sternly

"They are still bears," said Ms. Packer ~~sternest~~. "They are wild

respectful

animals and we need to be ~~respectest~~ of them."

Then Ms. Packer led the Outdoor Club members back to camp.

School-Home Connection Have the student add two sentences to the story. Each sentence should contain at least one word with the suffix -er, -est, -ly, or -ful.

Articles
Lesson 18

Name _____

▲ Use the articles *a*, *an*, and *the* to write two singular forms of each plural noun.

Examples: birds: a bird, the bird

icy roads: an icy road, the icy road

1. skyscrapers a skyscraper, the skyscraper

2. elevators an elevator, the elevator

3. rooftops a rooftop, the rooftop

4. noisy trains a noisy train, the noisy train

5. escalators an escalator, the escalator

6. shops a shop, the shop

7. airports an airport, the airport

8. excited boys an excited boy, the excited boy

9. red cars a red car, the red car

▲ Write a sentence for each article. Circle the article, and underline the noun that it introduces. Possible responses are shown.

10. a (A) boy walked his dog.

11. an I saw (an) elephant.

12. the It's fun to visit (the) big city.

Practice Book
© Harcourt • Grade 3

Prefixes un-, re-, dis-
Lesson 19

Name _____

Spelling Words

1. undo
2. redo
3. dislike
4. react
5. refill
6. uneasy
7. reread
8. unlike
9. remove
10. dishonest
11. unhappy
12. rebuild
13. displease
14. uncover
15. rewrite

▲ Sort and write the Spelling Words with the prefixes *un-* *re-* and *dis-*. Order may vary.

Words with Prefix *un-*

1. undo
2. uneasy
3. unlike
4. unhappy
5. uncover

Words with Prefix *re-*

6. redo
7. react
8. refill
9. reread
10. remove
11. rebuild
12. rewrite

Words with Prefix *dis-*

13. dislike
14. dishonest
15. displease

Practice Book
© Harcourt • Grade 3

▲ **Read the story. Then circle the letter of the best answer to each question.**

Nara the cat loved to daydream. She dreamed of living in a palace. She dreamed of wonderful meals and a servant to brush her fur. When her owner came near her, she hissed at him. She did not want to play. She just wanted to daydream.

The boy grew up and moved away, so Nara went to a new home. Nobody ever talked to her there. Nobody came to play with her, either. She had time to daydream, but she was not happy. She missed her old home. "I wish I had paid more attention to my owner," she thought. "We could have had fun. Now I am alone. My dreams were only dreams. Oh, why was I so foolish?"

1. What did Nara do instead of playing?
   A She ate and ate.
   B She ran away.
   C She slept in the sunshine.
   Ⓓ She dreamed of a different place.

2. How did Nara feel about her new home?
   A She was scared and nervous.
   Ⓑ She was unhappy.
   C She was happy and content.
   D She was cold and tired.

3. What is the theme of the story?
   Ⓐ Try to enjoy the life you have.
   B Daydreams are better than real life.
   C Always try to live in a palace.
   D Cats have unusual habits.

School–Home Connection
Talk about a story you have read with the student. What message did the author try to teach in the story?

▲ **Find the *un-* words in the Word Search. Look up, down, and across. Circle the words you find.**

u	j	u	n	c	o	v	e	r	l	i	a
n	u	s	u	n	p	l	a	n	n	e	d
s	a	t	r	c	l	a	i	e	o	n	m
u	n	c	o	o	k	e	d	w	u	a	n
r	u	p	v	w	r	q	e	z	h	h	u
e	n	u	n	c	r	o	s	s	h	n	n
s	d	l	t	o	h	r	u	n	a	r	r
f	o	m	b	r	t	f	n	l	p	i	e
l	i	h	a	i	g	p	w	a	p	o	a
e	u	n	r	o	l	l	i	n	y	e	d
u	n	l	o	c	k	t	s	o	r	b	f
x	t	o	k	d	y	v	e	u	k	m	s
e	y	b	v	i	u	n	e	a	t	e	n
u	n	a	b	l	e	u	n	c	a	p	j
u	n	c	o	m	m	o	n	x	c	w	a

School–Home Connection
With the student, think of things a person might do around their home that are spelled with the prefix *un-*. Write them in a list.

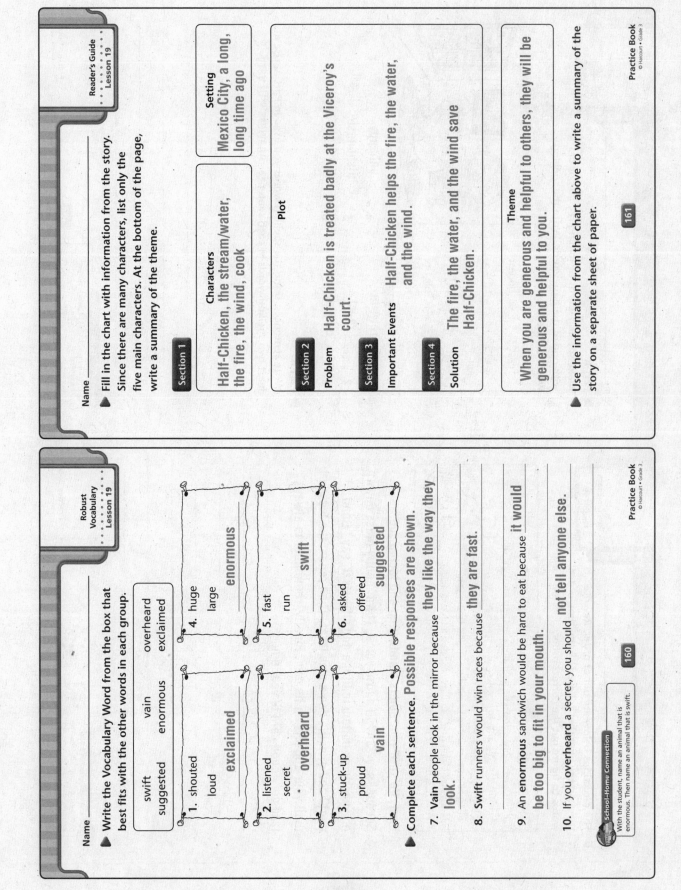

Name _____

▲ Fill in the chart with information from the story. Since there are many characters, list only the five main characters. At the bottom of the page, write a summary of the theme.

Setting

Mexico City, a long, long time ago

Characters

Half-Chicken, the stream/water, the fire, the wind, cook

Plot

Section 1

Section 2
Problem   Half-Chicken is treated badly at the Viceroy's court.

Section 3
Important Events   Half-Chicken helps the fire, the water, and the wind.

Section 4
Solution   The fire, the water, and the wind save Half-Chicken.

Theme

When you are generous and helpful to others, they will be generous and helpful to you.

▲ Use the information from the chart above to write a summary of the story on a separate sheet of paper.

161

Name _____

▲ Write the Vocabulary Word from the box that best fits with the other words in each group.

| swift | vain | overheard |
| suggested | enormous | exclaimed |

1. shouted
   loud
   exclaimed

2. listened
   secret
   overheard

3. stuck-up
   proud
   vain

4. huge
   large
   enormous

5. fast
   run
   swift

6. asked
   offered
   suggested

▲ Complete each sentence. Possible responses are shown.

7. Vain people look in the mirror because **they like the way they look.**

8. Swift runners would win races because **they are fast.**

9. An enormous sandwich would be hard to eat because **it would be too big to fit in your mouth.**

10. If you overheard a secret, you should **not tell anyone else.**

School-Home Connection
With the student, name an animal that is enormous. Then name an animal that is swift.

160

Name _____

▲ The directions below are out of order. Rewrite
them on the lines that follow. Use the time-order
words to figure out the correct order.

How to Teach a Dog to "Sit"

Third, gently press down on your dog's bottom until the dog sits.
Second, say "Sit" in a firm voice.
Then repeat the lesson until your dog sits on its own.
First, be sure your dog is standing up and facing you.
Next, say "Good dog!" and give the dog a nice treat.
Finally, remember to always take very good care of your dog.

First, be sure your dog is standing up and facing you.

Second, say "Sit" in a firm voice. Third, gently press down

on your dog's bottom until the dog sits. Next, say "Good

dog!" and give the dog a nice treat. Then repeat the lesson

until your dog sits on its own. Finally, remember to always

take very good care of your dog.

School-Home Connection
Have the student write directions for
something that he or she does every day.

162   Practice Book
© Harcourt • Grade 3

Name _____

▲ Part A
Make spelling words by joining re-, un-, or dis-
with one of the base words. Write the spelling
words on the lines.

re-	honest
	easy
un-	write
	act
dis-	please
	happy

1. rewrite   4. unhappy

2. react   5. dishonest

3. uneasy   6. displease

▲ Part B
Write sentences, using the spelling words you used in Part A. Use at
least two spelling words in each sentence. Answers will vary.

7. _____

8. _____

9. _____

School-Home Connection
With the student, think of other words with
the prefixes re-, un-, and dis-. Write the words
in a list.

163   Practice Book
© Harcourt • Grade 3

© Harcourt • Grade 3   **Student Edition** pp. 162–163

Name _____

▲ Rewrite each sentence. Use the correct form of the verb in parentheses ( ).

1. An egg (hatch/hatches) in the nest.
   An egg hatches in the nest.

2. The ducklings (follow/follows) their mother.
   The ducklings follow their mother.

3. The farmer (hurry/hurries) home.
   The farmer hurries home.

4. Mice (scurry/scurries) around the barn.
   Mice scurry around the barn.

5. We (milk/milks) the cows every morning.
   We milk the cows every morning.

6. She (drive/drives) the big tractor.
   She drives the big tractor.

7. Jessica (help/helps) my brother dry dishes.
   Jessica helps my brother dry dishes.

8. They (clean/cleans) the kitchen.
   They clean the kitchen.

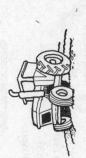

School-Home Connection
Work with your child to write four sentences, using action verbs in the present tense. Ask him or her to underline each verb and write S (singular) or P (plural) above each subject.

Name _____

▲ Read the words in the Word Box. Write each word in the correct column. Then answer the questions.

pour	wore	swarm	score	board
hoarse	horse	warp	before	port
wart	roar	fort	course	four

r-controlled vowel pattern:

or	ore	our	ar	oar
port	wore	pour	swarm	board
fort	score	course	wart	hoarse
horse	before	four	warp	roar

1. How are the words *pour* and *hour* alike and different?
   Possible response: They both have the letter pattern *our,* **but they are pronounced differently.**

2. What other words use *ore* to make the /ôr/ sound?
   Possible responses: more, shore, bore, core, before, adore, pore

3. What is one more word with *ar* that stands for /ôr/? What is one word with *ar* that does not stand for /ôr/?
   Possible responses: warm, farm

School-Home Connection
Ask the student to think of one more word for each column of the chart.

Name _____

▲ Fold the paper along the dotted line. As each spelling word is read aloud, write it in the blank. Then unfold your paper and check your work. Practice writing any spelling words you missed.

Spelling Words

1. form
2. wore
3. fourth
4. soar
5. warm
6. perfect
7. girl
8. burn
9. work
10. earth
11. bigger
12. finest
13. lonely
14. refill
15. dishonest

1. _____
2. _____
3. _____
4. _____
5. _____
6. _____
7. _____
8. _____
9. _____
10. _____
11. _____
12. _____
13. _____
14. _____
15. _____

Review
r-Controlled Vowel:
/ûr/er, ir, ur,
ir, or, ear
Lesson 20

Name _____

▲ Circle the word in each clue that has the /ûr/ sound. Then write the circled words in the crossword puzzle.

Across

1. I like the purple pants.
4. Help me search for my dog.
6. Make a left turn.
7. Have you memorized all the spelling words?

Down

1. That is a pretty pearl necklace.
2. We will learn about vowels today.
3. I want to buy new shirts.
5. Chopping wood is hard work.

School-Home Connection

Ask the student to think of other words that use er, ir, ur, or, and ear to stand for the /ûr/ sound. Help the student make sentences that include several of these words.

Name _____

▲ Read the passage. Then compare and contrast frogs and toads by completing the chart.
Possible responses are shown.

Frogs and Toads

Although frogs and toads are similar, they are also quite different. Frogs and toads are both amphibians. They live both in water and on land, hatching from eggs as tadpoles. Both creatures can make sounds by passing air through their throats. Both also have special glands on their skin that make their bodies taste bad to predators.

Frogs, however, have moist, smooth skin, while toads have drier, bumpy skin. In addition, frogs have longer back legs and can jump higher and farther than toads can jump. But toads can walk. Frogs also have tiny teeth, but toads have no teeth at all.

Next time you see a frog, stop and look. It could be a toad!

Frogs only	Frogs and Toads	Toads only
• moist, smooth skin	• amphibians	• dry, bumpy skin
• long back legs	• live in water and on land	• hop shorter distances than frogs, and can walk
• jump high and far	• hatch from eggs as tadpoles	• no teeth
• tiny teeth	• make sounds with their throats	
	• taste bad to predators	

School-Home Connection
Have the student name two of his or her favorite animals and write sentences comparing and contrasting them.

Name _____

▲ Read this part of a student's rough draft. Then answer the questions that follow.

(1) There was an art show at the library yesterday. (2) Children displayed their art. (3) I showed two paintings. (4) They were the largest ones in the room. (5) There were also _____ photographs and a black sculpture. (6) The sculpture was interesting than the photographs.

1. Which sentence uses the correct form of an adjective that compares?
A Sentence 3
B Sentence 4
C Sentence 5
D Sentence 6

2. Which adjective needs the word *more* before it?
A two (Sentence 3)
B largest (Sentence 4)
C black (Sentence 5)
D interesting (Sentence 6)

3. Which adjective could be written before *Children* in Sentence 2?
A Many
B One
C Hundred
D Each

4. Which adjective that tells *what kind* could fill in the blank in Sentence 5?
A biggest
B tiniest
C small
D some

5. Which sentence has an adjective that tells *what color?*
A Sentence 1
B Sentence 3
C Sentence 4
D Sentence 5

6. Which of these sentences does NOT have an adjective?
A Sentence 2
B Sentence 3
C Sentence 4
D Sentence 5

Name _____

▲ Underline the prefix or suffix in each word.
Then write the meaning of the word.

Word	Definition
1. repay	to pay again
2. joyful	full of joy
3. unwrap	to take the wrap off
4. colder	more cold
5. disrespect	to not respect
6. funniest	the most funny
7. unable	not able
8. eventful	full of events
9. cleverly	in a way that is clever
10. happiest	the most happy

Practice Book
© Harcourt • Grade 3

171

Name _____

▲ Circle the word in each row that is spelled
incorrectly. Then write the correct word on
the line.

1. lovely	loveler	loveliest	lovelier
2. fast	faster	fastiest	fastest
3. nicer	niciest	nicely	nicest
4. biggier	biggest	big	bigger
5. clumsy	clumsest	clumsier	clumsiest
6. hardder	hardly	hardest	harder
7. quietly	quietier	quietest	quieter
8. softtest	softly	softer	softest
9. sillyer	silliest	silly	sillier
10. gentle	gentler	gentliest	gentlest

Practice Book
© Harcourt • Grade 3

170

Student Edition pp. 170–171

Robust Vocabulary
Lesson 20

Name _____

▲ Use the clues to unscramble the letters. Then write the Vocabulary Word and definition.

| versions | rehearse | mandatory |
| criticize | immerse | dialogue |

1. Soccer practice is ytdnamaro if you want to play in the game.
mandatory – required

2. When you rrheeesa for the play, make sure you say your lines clearly.
rehearse – to practice

3. Many painters sketch out different nsovreis before they begin painting.
versions – different drafts of something.

4. When teachers zicitrcei your work, they give you suggestions to improve it.
criticize – to tell what can be changed about something

5. The best way to learn about something is to emmeisr yourself in it.
immerse – to surround yourself

6. The eulaodig in a book can tell you a lot about a character's traits.
dialogue – a conversation

Practice Book
© Harcourt • Grade 3

School–Home Connection
Have the student make up other sentences using the Vocabulary Words.

Name _____

● Circle the word that matches the definition. Then underline the other words that are real words.

1. to take off the cover
discover   (uncover)   recover

2. to play again
(replay)   unplay   display

3. to visit again
disvisit   unvisit   (revisit)

4. to not like something
unlike   (dislike)   relike

5. to type again
(retype)   distype   untype

6. not popular
repopular   dispopular   (unpopular)

7. to not obey
(disobey)   reobey   unobey

School–Home Connection
Ask the student to reread the word choices for #4 and share a definition for *unlike*. Point out that, in this case, *like* is an adjective.

Practice Book
© Harcourt • Grade 3

▲ Read this part of a student's rough draft.
Then answer the questions that follow.

(1) Luke interviews his mother for a newsletter at school. (2) He
asks his mother questions and writes down a answers. (3) _____
questions are about his mother's job. (4) Luke's mother is a engineer.
(5) She plans bridges, and people builds them. (6) Students enjoy the
report that Luke writes.

1. In which sentence should the
   article be changed to *an*?
   A Sentence 1
   B Sentence 2
   C Sentence 4
   D Sentence 6

2. Which word could fill in the
   blank in Sentence 3?
   A A
   B An
   C The
   D Writes

3. Which sentence has a plural
   noun with an article that does
   NOT agree?
   A Sentence 1
   B Sentence 2
   C Sentence 4
   D Sentence 6

4. Which of these action verbs
   does NOT agree with its
   subject?
   A interviews (Sentence 1)
   B writes (Sentence 2)
   C plans (Sentence 5)
   D builds (Sentence 5)

5. Which sentence has only one
   action verb?
   A Sentence 1
   B Sentence 2
   C Sentence 5
   D Sentence 6

6. Which sentence has a plural
   subject and an action verb that
   agrees?
   A Sentence 1
   B Sentence 2
   C Sentence 4
   D Sentence 6

▲ Read the story. Then answer the questions.
Possible responses are shown.

Olivia wanted to be a singer more than anything in the world.
"Your voice is too scratchy and low," Carl said during choir practice.
"It sounds like you ate a cactus!"

Olivia tried to ignore him. Her voice did not sound like the other
singers' voices. Carl's voice was smooth and not too high or too low.

"I have new songs today," Miss Cuttle announced to the class. "Each
person will get a song to sing that suits his or her voice."

Olivia was nervous. She wondered what song could suit her rough
voice. Olivia anxiously walked up to Miss Cuttle. "I know I have
problems with my voice," Olivia said quietly.

Miss Cuttle grinned. "I have a special song for you. Many famous
jazz singers had voices just like yours. I think a jazz song will be perfect."

1. What is Olivia's voice like? rough and low

2. Why is Olivia nervous? She wonders what song could suit
her voice.

3. Why does Miss Cuttle choose a jazz song for Olivia? Many famous
jazz singers had voices just like Olivia's.

4. What is one possible theme for the story? Everyone can use the
talents he or she has.

School-Home Connection
Have the student explain which story clues he
or she used to determine the story's theme.

Review: Follow Directions — Lesson 20

Name _____

▲ **Follow the directions to draw a picture in the space below.**

First, draw a square.

Second, draw a large circle inside the square.

Third, draw two triangles inside the circle.

Fourth, draw a star below the triangles.

Last, write the names of all the shapes you drew below the picture.

Possible drawing is shown. Check students' work and accept any drawings that follow the directions.

Shapes: **square, circle, triangles, star**

Practice Book
© Harcourt • Grade 3

176

Vowel Variants /ōō/ oo, ew, ue, ui; /ŏŏ/ oo — Lesson 21

Spelling Words

1. threw
2. cool
3. foot
4. cook
5. bruise
6. hook
7. tool
8. brook
9. booth
10. school
11. choose
12. balloon
13. cartoon
14. afternoon
15. understood

Name _____

▲ **Read the Spelling Words. Then write each word in the group where it belongs. Order may vary.**

Words with /ōō/ as in booth

1. threw
2. cool
3. bruise
4. booth
5. school
6. choose
7. balloon
8. cartoon
9. afternoon
10. tool

Words with /ŏŏ/ as in cook

11. foot
12. cook
13. hook
14. brook

▲ **Write the word that is left on the line.**

15. understood

Practice Book
© Harcourt

177

91

Student Edition pp. 176–177

Name _____

▲ Circle the /o͞o/ word in each riddle. Then unscramble the letters to make a /o͞o/ word that solves the riddle. Write the answer word on the line.

What Am I?

1. I am a place where you might see a (kangaroo).

   ozo _____ **zoo**

2. You do this when you eat (food).

   wche _____ **chew**

3. I am a building with many (classrooms).

   socohl _____ **school**

4. It's hard to eat (noodles) while using me.

   nospo _____ **spoon**

5. Someone did this to make a (cartoon).

   rewd _____ **drew**

School-Home Connection
Work with the student to create another /o͞o/ riddle with *moon*, *flew*, or *new*.

179

Practice Book
© Harcourt • Grade 3

Name _____

▲ Read the passage and answer the questions.

Roald Amundsen (1872–1928) was a polar explorer from Norway. He is best known for leading the first successful expedition to the South Pole, which lasted from 1910 to 1912.

Before leading his own expedititons, Amundsen was a member of the Belgian Antarctic Expedition (1897–1899). This journey taught Amundsen how to survive the harshness of Antarctica. He would later use this knowledge for his own expeditions.

In 1910, Amundsen and his expedition set out for the South Pole. On his ship *Fram*, whose name means "forward," Amundsen and his crew first arrived at the edge of the Ross Ice Shelf. There he established a base camp, from which he led his crew across the Antarctic ice. Amundsen and his crew arrived at the South Pole on December 14, 1911. Then they faced the long, dangerous journey back. It took until March 1, 1912, to complete that trek and let the rest of the world hear the news of their accomplishment.

1. What happened before Amundsen led his own expeditions?
   He was a member of the Belgian Antarctic Expedition.

2. When did Amundsen begin his journey to the South Pole?
   in 1910

3. When did Amundsen and his crew arrive at the South Pole?
   on December 14, 1911

4. What are some time-order words used in this passage?
   Possible responses: Before, later, in 1910, first, on December 14, 1911, then, until March 1, 1912

School-Home Connection
Help the student write sentences explaining a trip he or she would like to take. Use time-order words, like *first* and *next*, to explain steps in order.

178

Practice Book
© Harcourt • Grade 3

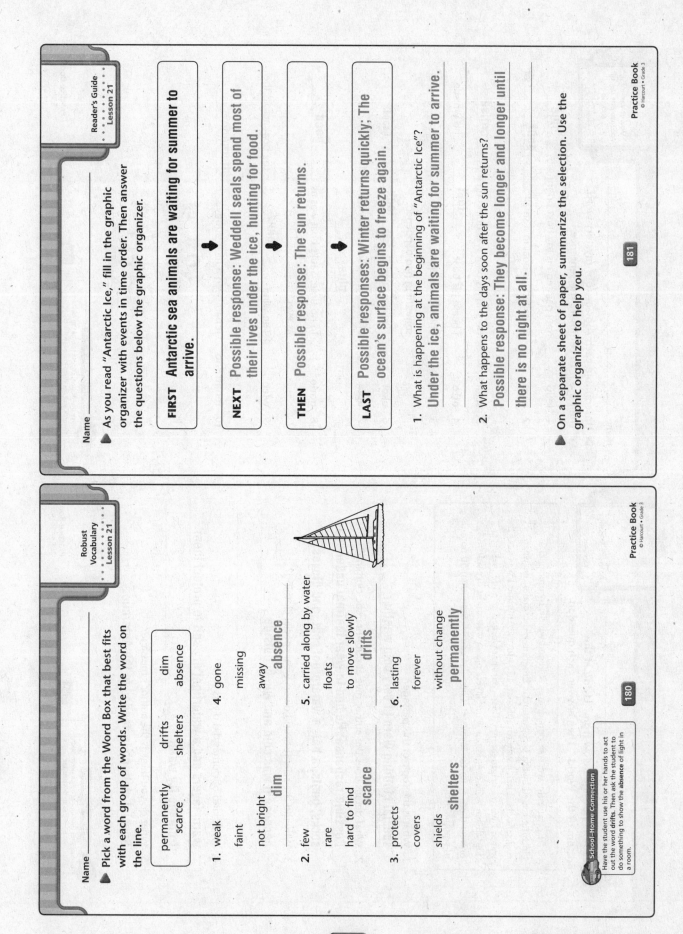

Name _____

Robust Vocabulary
Lesson 21

▲ Pick a word from the Word Box that best fits with each group of words. Write the word on the line.

| permanently | drifts | dim |
| scarce | shelters | absence |

1. weak
   faint
   not bright
   dim

2. few
   rare
   hard to find
   scarce

3. protects
   covers
   shields
   shelters

4. gone
   missing
   away
   absence

5. carried along by water
   floats
   to move slowly
   drifts

6. lasting
   forever
   without change
   permanently

School-Home Connection
Have the student use his or her hands to act out the word **drifts**. Then ask the student to do something to show the **absence** of light in a room.

Practice Book
© Harcourt • Grade 3

Name _____

Reader's Guide
Lesson 21

▲ As you read "Antarctic Ice," fill in the graphic organizer with events in time order. Then answer the questions below the graphic organizer.

FIRST Antarctic sea animals are waiting for summer to arrive.

↓

NEXT Possible response: Weddell seals spend most of their lives under the ice, hunting for food.

↓

THEN Possible response: The sun returns.

↓

LAST Possible responses: Winter returns quickly; The ocean's surface begins to freeze again.

1. What is happening at the beginning of "Antarctic Ice"?
   Under the ice, animals are waiting for summer to arrive.

2. What happens to the days soon after the sun returns?
   Possible response: They become longer and longer until there is no night at all.

▲ On a separate sheet of paper, summarize the selection. Use the graphic organizer to help you.

Practice Book
© Harcourt • Grade 3

Student Edition pp. 180–181

Left page (182)

Name _____

▲ Read the passage below from "Living at the Bottom of the World." Then answer each question.

Because the weather outside was cold and windy, I wore special clothing issued by the U.S. Antarctic Program—thermal underwear, socks, boots, a hat, a waterproof coat, and gloves. Anytime I was near the water, I wore a bright-orange float-coat that worked as a life preserver. The divers wore even more warm layers plus a watertight dry suit to protect them from the icy water. They also carried more than 50 pounds of equipment.

1. What is the topic of this passage?

   special clothing worn in very cold weather

2. What details does the author give about Antarctic clothing?

   Possible response: He had to wear thermal underwear,

   socks, boots, a hat, a waterproof coat, and gloves.

3. Why did the scientists and divers wear special clothing?

   because it was cold and windy outside

4. What kind of clothes did divers wear?

   warm layers and a watertight dry suit to protect them

   from the icy water

5. What do you think is the author's message?

   Special clothing is needed in the Antarctic.

School-Home Connection
Discuss with the student other information that might be added to this passage.

182

Right page (183)

Name _____

▲ Unscramble each /ōō/ or /ŏŏ/ mystery word. Then use it to complete the sentence.

1. leub   Saul painted his toy boat bright blue .

2. olop   He sailed his boat in a small pool of water.

3. sciure   He said his boat was going on a cruise .

4. otto   I heard his boat toot and whistle.

5. nwek   Then it was quiet, and I knew something had happened.

6. okol   "Let me take a look ," I said.

7. ugle   I fixed the broken boat with a little bit of glue .

8. godo   In no time, Saul's boat was as good as ever.

9. wleb   The wind blew the boat across the water.

10. fenatrono It had been a nice, sunny afternoon .

183

School-Home Connection
Have the student choose two of the mystery words and use them in oral sentences.

94

The Verb Be
Lesson 21

Name _____

▲ Circle the form of the verb *be* in each sentence. Then write whether each links the subject to words that tell *what* or *where*.

1. Some seals (are) white. ___ what

2. The penguin chick (was) fuzzy. ___ what

3. You (were) on the shore. ___ where

4. That shark (is) near a whale. ___ where

5. I (am) with my parents. ___ where

6. They (are) scientists. ___ what

▲ Rewrite each sentence, using a correct form of the verb *be*. Then write *S* above each singular subject and *P* above each plural subject. **Possible responses are shown.**

7. Those fish ___ small and silver.
   P
   Those fish are small and silver.

8. We ___ close to the beaver's dam.
   P
   We were close to the beaver's dam.

9. He ___ in a wooden boat.
   S
   He was in a wooden boat.

10. The river ___ full of life.
    S
    The river is full of life.

School-Home Connection
Have your child write sentences about his or her favorite season. Ask him or her to use singular and plural subjects and to write sentences that tell *what* and *where*.

Vowel Variants
/ô/ o, au, aw, a(l), au(gh), ough
Lesson 22

Name _____

▲ Read the Spelling Words. Listen for the vowel sound in each word. Sort the words and write them where they belong.

Spelling Words

1. ought
2. soft
3. yawn
4. walk
5. long
6. also
7. thaw
8. lost
9. cause
10. taught
11. pause
12. straw
13. false
14. author
15. almost

Words Beginning with a Vowel Sound

1. also
2. author
3. almost
4. ought

Words with a Vowel Sound in the Middle

5. soft
6. yawn
7. walk
8. long
9. lost
10. cause
11. taught
12. pause
13. false
14. thaw
15. straw

School-Home Connection
With your child, make a list of words that have the same vowel sound you hear in the word *ball*. Discuss the spelling of each word.

Name _____

▲ Read the article. Then write the main events in order.

Fishing With Feet

One kind of bat eats fish. The way the bat catches its dinner is amazing. First, it flies very low over the water. Next, it dangles its hind legs in the water. The legs look like a tasty treat to the fish, so the fish comes closer. Then, the bat snags a small fish with its sharp toenails. The fish may struggle, but the bat holds tight. Finally, the bat pulls the fish out of the water and eats it.

First The bat flies low over the water. _____

Next The bat dangles its hind legs in the water. _____

Then The bat catches a fish with its toe nails. _____

Finally The bat eats the fish. _____

School-Home Connection
With the student, watch an animal in your community. Have the student describe what the animal does, using time-order words.

Practice Book
© Harcourt • Grade 3

Name _____

▲ In the chart below, write a word from the Word Box in the correct column. Some words might belong in more than one column. Use the words that do not belong in any column to answer the questions below.

ought	soar	caught	pause
clown	bought	cause	strong
author	cool	boil	taught

Words with /ô/ as au	Words with /ô/ as ou	Words with gh
taught	ought	ought
cause	bought	taught
pause		bought
caught		caught
author		

1. How would a glass of lemonade feel on a hot summer day?
cool

2. If you could lift a heavy load of books, what would you be?
strong

3. What happens to water when it heats until bubbles appear?
boil

4. What kind of person is very funny and usually wears a big red nose?
clown

5. What does a bird do when it flies high into the air? soar

School-Home Connection
With the student, think of other words that have /ô/ as au. Have him or her write the words in sentences.

Practice Book
© Harcourt • Grade 3

© Harcourt • Grade 3

Student Edition pp. 186–187

▲ Write the Vocabulary Word from the box that goes with each explanation.

| effort | swoops | detail |
| fluttering | nocturnal | dozes |

1. __nocturnal__   Active at night

2. __detail__   An important point

3. __swoops__   Flies quickly downward

4. __effort__   Trying hard

5. __fluttering__   Moving wings quickly

6. __dozes__   Sleeps lightly

▲ Answer the questions in complete sentences. Possible responses are shown.

7. If a bird **swoops**, does it move quickly or slowly?
A bird that swoops moves quickly.

8. If you notice a **detail** in a painting, are you looking at only a part of it?
You see a detail if you are looking at part of the painting.

9. If someone makes an **effort**, is he or she trying hard or not trying?
A person who makes an effort is trying hard.

10. When is a **nocturnal** animal likely to be active?
A nocturnal animal is active at night.

11. Is it hard or easy to wake up someone who **dozes**?
It is easy to wake up someone who dozes.

12. If a bird is **fluttering**, how are its wings moving?
When a bird is fluttering, its wings are moving very quickly.

School-Home Connection
With the student, look outside for **nocturnal** animals and insects that might be **fluttering** around an outside light at night.

188

Practice Book
© Harcourt • Grade 3

▲ As you read "Bat Loves the Night," fill in the graphic organizer with the sequence of events in the narrative. Possible responses are shown.

FIRST

Bat wakes up, spreads her wings, and flies.

→

NEXT

Bat hears a moth and tries to catch it. It gets away at first, but then she catches it and eats it.

→

THEN

Night draws to an end, and Bat flies back to her roost. Her baby waits there.

→

LAST

Bat dozes with her baby, waiting for the night.

1. What happens to the moth after Bat bites it for the first time?
It gets away, but Bat catches it again.

2. What is the last thing Bat does in the narrative?
She goes to sleep.

▲ On a separate sheet of paper, summarize the selection. Use the graphic organizer to help you. Answers will vary.

Name _____

▲ Read the passage. Circle the letter of the best answer to each question about the author's message.

Many people know that baseball is called "America's pastime" because it is so popular in the United States. But did you know that another game that uses a bat and a ball is just as popular in other parts of the world? That game is cricket, and a lot of its rules are similar to baseball's. Cricket is played with two teams. Each team takes turns batting and fielding, like in baseball.

In baseball, the batter stands at home plate. In cricket, a player called a striker stands at a spot called a wicket. In baseball, the player who throws the ball is called the pitcher; in cricket, that player is called the bowler. Both games have umpires. Cricket has been played since the 1300s and is still popular all over the world today!

1. How is cricket like baseball?
   A Both games have catchers.
   B Both games use a bat and a ball.
   C Both games have players called shortstops.
   D Both games use wickets.

2. Which sentence is true?
   A Both cricket and baseball have pitchers.
   B Cricket uses umpires, but baseball does not.
   C Cricket is played with four teams; baseball is played with two.
   D Cricket has been played since the 1300's, but baseball was invented in the 1800s.

3. What was the author's message in this passage?
   A Cricket is popular in the United States.
   B Baseball players should play cricket instead.
   C Playing cricket or baseball is a good way to get in shape.
   D Cricket and baseball are alike and different in many ways.

School-Home Connection
Ask the student to point out some of the sentences that helped show the author's message in this selection.

190

Name _____

▲ Write the words from the word box in the correct column. Then, find the /ô/ words in the word search below.

bought	caught	taught
fought	ought	author
thought	pause	

/ô/ as au(gh)	/ô/ as ough
taught	thought
caught	bought
author	fought
pause	ought

WORD SEARCH

B	F	T	A	U	G	H	T	X	A
D	P	A	U	S	E	I	H	U	A
F	Q	I	T	R	C	J	O	V	R
O	U	G	H	T	A	T	U	C	I
U	R	H	O	C	A	U	G	H	T
G	S	K	R	Z	W	E	H	U	N
H	M	B	O	U	G	H	T	A	W
T	G	E	O	H	K	N	A	L	T

191

School-Home Connection
With the student, talk about the different sounds au(gh) and ough make. List other words that have those sounds.

Main and Helping Verbs
Lesson 22

Name _____

▲ Rewrite the sentences. Add a helping verb to each one. **Possible responses are shown.**

1. I never studied mammals.
   I have never studied mammals.

2. We learn about bats.
   We will learn about bats.

3. We go to the library.
   We should go to the library.

4. Butterflies see red, yellow, and green.
   Butterflies can see red, yellow, and green.

5. A butterfly landed on that leaf.
   A butterfly has landed on that leaf.

6. That butterfly laid 400 eggs.
   That butterfly has laid 400 eggs.

7. Butterflies fly only when they are warm.
   Butterflies will fly only when they are warm.

8. The librarian found a great book about butterflies.
   The librarian has found a great book about butterflies.

School-Home Connection
Work with your child to write four sentences about nighttime that include main and helping verbs. Have your child underline each main verb and circle each helping verb.

Practice Book
© Harcourt • Grade 3

Prefix pre-, mis-, in-
Lesson 23

Name _____

▲ Read the Spelling Words. Sort the words and write them where they belong.

Spelling Words
1. input
2. preset
3. misuse
4. inside
5. preview
6. incorrect
7. pretest
8. mislead
9. preheat
10. indoors
11. misplace
12. preschool
13. misread
14. mismatch
15. misspell

Words with pre-

1. preset
2. preview
3. pretest
4. preheat
5. preschool

Words with mis-

6. misuse
7. mislead
8. misplace
9. misread
10. mismatch
11. misspell

Words with in-

12. input
13. inside
14. incorrect
15. indoors

School-Home Connection
With your child, make a list of five words with the prefixes pre-, mis-, and in-. Then have your child circle the prefix in each word. Challenge him or her to use each word in a sentence.

Practice Book
© Harcourt • Grade 3

Student Edition pp. 192–193

Name _____

▲ Read the passage. Look for cause and effect relationships as you read. Then answer the questions.

Using Good Sense

Bats are amazing creatures. Not only are they the only flying mammals, but they also have great senses. Bats have strong senses of smell, hearing, and eyesight. Because of these great senses, bats are able to be active at night.

Bats use their hearing, vision, and sense of smell to find food in the dark. In fact, they can see better in the dark than in the daylight. Their strong sense of smell lets bats find ripe fruit. They use their sharp hearing to find other food sources, too, such as insects and fish.

Bats also use these strong senses to find other bats. They use their sense of smell to recognize their roost mates. Their great hearing helps them find their young.

1. What causes bats to be able to be active at night?
   Possible response: Their sense of hearing, smell, and sight.

2. What is an effect of a bat's strong sense of hearing?
   Possible response: They can find insects and fish.

3. What causes bats to be able to find other bats?
   Possible response: hearing and smell

4. What is an effect of a bat's strong sense of smell?
   Possible response: They can find ripening fruit.

School-Home Connection
Read and discuss the passage with the student. Have him or her explain the cause and effect relationships in the text using words such as so and because.

194

Practice Book
© Harcourt • Grade 3

Name _____

▲ Look at the words in the squares. Shade the squares that have words with the prefix pre-, mis-, or in- in front of a root word. Circle the prefix in each word.

preheat	pretzel	misuse	preview
injure	mister	pretest	indoors
predator	misspell	miserable	insect
input	preschool	mislead	ink
missing	president	incorrect	mission

School-Home Connection
Have the student read the spelling words on the page aloud. Then ask him or her to share the meanings of the words with the prefix pre-.

195

Practice Book
© Harcourt • Grade 3

Name _____

| fondness | decent | inherit |
| ridiculous | emotion | disgraceful |

▲ Part A. Write the Vocabulary Word that matches each idea.

1. __ridiculous__ ___ something silly or strange

2. __decent__ ___ honest and good

3. __inherit__ ___ to receive something from someone else

4. __fondness__ ___ a liking or affection

5. __disgraceful__ ___ shameful or unacceptable

6. __emotion__ ___ a feeling such as happiness or anger

▲ Part B. Answer each question about the Vocabulary Words.

7. If someone's actions are **disgraceful**, should that person be embarrassed by or proud of that behavior?
__embarrassed__

8. Would a **decent** person be trustworthy or untrustworthy?
__trustworthy__

9. Would something **ridiculous** make you laugh or cry?
__laugh__

10. What kind of **emotion** would make you smile?
__a happy emotion__

11. Would a mouse have a **fondness** for snakes or cheese?
__cheese__

12. If you **inherit** something, is it a gift or do you buy it?
__a gift__

School–Home Connection

Ask the student to give examples of things that are ridiculous. Then ask him or her to name several emotions and to tell which things cause those feelings.

Name _____

▲ As you read "Chestnut Cove," fill in the graphic organizer. Sometimes there may be more than one cause or effect for a single action. You may also find more than one cause and effect relationship in the story. Draw more boxes as you need them.

Possible responses are shown.

| Section 1 | page 233 |

Cause
The fish drank the pond.

→ **Effect**
Everyone helped move the fish to the lake.

Effect
The villagers began to change.

| Section 2 | page 238 |

Cause
watermelon-growing contest

Effect
The villagers didn't talk to each other as much.

Effect
Some villagers built fences.

1. What was one cause you found in the story?
Possible response: The king announced the watermelon contest.

2. What effect or effects did this action have?
Answers will vary, but should support the cause listed in the response to Question 1.

▲ On a separate sheet of paper, summarize the selection. Use the graphic organizer to help you. **Answers will vary.**

Name _____

▲ Choose the correct homophone to complete each sentence. Then write a sentence using the other homophone.

1. blew / blue

We painted my bedroom walls __blue__

Possible response: The wind blew during the storm.

2. pear / pair

I wore a new __pair__ of shoes to school today.

Possible response: I ate a pear with my lunch.

3. see / sea

The sailor said there is nothing like being on the open __sea__

Possible response: We can see the playground from our house.

4. nose / knows

Do you think anyone __knows__ how to get there?

Possible response: My nose itches.

5. hair / hare

She washes her __hair__ every night.

Possible response: The tortoise finished the race before the hare.

School–Home Connection
Have the student write homophones for bee, won, knight, two, and their.

Name _____

▲ Read each of the words at the top of the page. Then follow the directions below.

precook   mislead

invisible   preheat

mismatch   prepackage   misuse

1. Circle the word that means "to package before."

2. Draw a triangle around the word that means "not visible."

3. Underline the word that means "to cook before."

4. Draw a box around the word that means "to use badly."

5. Cross off the word the means "to lead wrongly."

6. Draw a star beside the word that means "to heat before."

7. Draw a zigzag line under the word that means "to match wrongly."

School–Home Connection
Have the student use the words invisible, preheat, and misdirect in sentences. Then ask him or her to tell you the meanings of each of the prefixes.

Present-Tense Verbs
Lesson 23

Name _____

▲ Rewrite each sentence correctly, using the subject in parentheses ( ). Be sure that the verb in your sentence agrees with its new subject.

Example: Glenda likes math. (My brothers)
<u>My brothers like math.</u>

1. I enter a writing contest. (George)
<u>George enters a writing contest.</u>

2. The teachers judge the contest. (A teacher)
<u>A teacher judges the contest.</u>

3. One student wins the contest. (Two students)
<u>Two students win the contest.</u>

4. We like stories about animals. (You)
<u>You like stories about animals.</u>

5. She prefers true stories. (He)
<u>He prefers true stories.</u>

6. The princesses meet a prince. (The princess)
<u>The princess meets a prince.</u>

7. We hurry home from school. (They)
<u>They hurry home from school.</u>

8. Our mother opens the front door. (We)
<u>We open the front door.</u>

School-Home Connection
Write two sentences with present-tense verbs. Ask your child to rewrite the sentences, changing the subjects and making sure that the verbs agree with their new subjects.

Practice Book
© Harcourt • Grade 3
200

Schwa /ə/
Lesson 24

Name _____

▲ Read the Spelling Words. Sort the words and write them where they belong. **Order may vary.**

Spelling Words
1. upon
2. above
3. cover
4. apart
5. either
6. alike
7. awake
8. afraid
9. across
10. agree
11. ever
12. amount
13. ahead
14. alive
15. around

Words Beginning with the /ə/ Sound
1. upon
2. above
3. apart
4. alike
5. awake
6. afraid
7. agree
8. amount
9. alive
10. across
11. ahead
12. around

Words Ending with the /ər/ Sound
13. cover
14. ever
15. either

School-Home Connection
Brainstorm with your child other words that have the schwa sound that you hear in *above* and *ever*. Discuss how to spell each word. Confirm each spelling in a dictionary.

Practice Book
© Harcourt • Grade 3
201

Cause and Effect
Lesson 24

▲ **Read the passage. Then answer the questions.**
Possible responses are shown.

"Ha!" Keisha said. "I knew I could do it!" Keisha had just taught herself to ride her older brother, Ben's, bike. Ben had delivered papers for six months and made enough money to buy it. He told her not to ride the bike because she was too little and might break it. Since she was stubborn, Keisha secretly rode the bike when he was at oboe practice.

One afternoon, Keisha left the bike on the driveway and went inside. Then she heard a loud crunch from outside. "Oh no!" she said. "The bike!" Sure enough, Mom had run over the bike with the car. Since the broken bike was Keisha's fault, she agreed to help Ben deliver newspapers on foot until he made enough money to buy a new bike.

1. What is the cause of Keisha secretly riding Ben's bike?
   She is stubborn.

2. What is the effect of Keisha leaving the bike on the driveway?
   Mom runs over it with the car.

3. What is the cause of Keisha helping Ben deliver newspapers?
   The broken bike is her fault.

4. What is the effect of Ben delivering papers for six months?
   He will make enough money to buy a new bike.

School-Home Connection
Ask the student to identify the cause of Ben telling Keisha not to ride his bike.

202

Practice Book
© Harcourt • Grade 3

Schwa
Lesson 24

▲ **Read the incomplete sentences below. Underline the word that has the schwa sound and completes the sentence.**

1. If you do not understand the sentence, read _____. (ahead / slowly)

2. After the race, she needed to drink a lot of _____. (water / limeade)

3. The building in the _____ is the tallest. (background / center)

4. The school play was a huge _____. (success / sellout)

5. A long time _____, my family lived in Italy. (back / ago)

6. My sister has special _____ because she is a runner. (outfits / sneakers)

7. They went _____ on vacation to the Grand Canyon. (away / quickly)

8. What was your _____ for being late? (excuse / reason)

9. She had to do her math homework _____ because she made too many mistakes. (twice / again)

10. Autumn is my favorite _____ because of the colorful leaves. (season / time)

School-Home Connection
Ask the student to identify the letters that make the schwa sound in items #1 and #2.

203

Practice Book
© Harcourt • Grade 3

Name _____

▲ Part A. Choose one Vocabulary Word from the box to complete each unfinished sentence below. Write the word on the line.

| clutter | mentioned | remark |
| visible | beckoned | flustered |

Anna's mom entered her daughter's room. It was a mess! Anna's bed was so covered with clothes, it was barely **visible** _____. Anna's mom _____ **mentioned** that perhaps Anna should clean her room if she wanted to play with her friends. Anna seemed **flustered** _____, but she did start putting things away. About an hour later, Anna _____ **beckoned** to her mom to take a look. All the _____ **clutter** had been removed. Her mom was pleased with the results. Anna was able to go out and play. As she ran out the door, Anna heard her mom _____ **remark** , "Good job!"

▲ Part B. Write one or two sentences to answer each question.

1. What might you show your friends if you *beckoned* for them to come see something?
   Possible response: I might show them a pretty bird I saw in a tree.

2. How would you make sure you were *visible* if you were riding your bicycle at night?
   Possible responses: I would wear reflectors; I would get a bike light.

School-Home Connection
Ask the student to think of three things that would make them feel *flustered*.

Practice Book
© Harcourt • Grade 3

Name _____

▲ As you read "Ramona Quimby, Age 8," think about events that cause other events to happen. Think about events that happen as a result of others. Write the causes and effects in the chart below. **Possible responses are shown.**

Section 1 pages 262–263

Cause
Ramona is home sick from school.

➔

Effect
She watches a lot of TV commercials.

Section 2 pages 264–267

Cause
Ramona has lots of ideas.

➔

Effect
She prints them rather than wasting time writing in cursive.

Section 3 pages 268–271

Cause
Ramona cannot remember the end to her book report.

➔

Effect
She says "I can't believe I read the whole thing!"

1. How does Ramona choose to present her book report? **She and her friends put on a show like the commercials she watched.**

2. What causes this to happen? **She wants her book report to be different from everyone else's.**

▲ On a separate sheet of paper, summarize "Ramona Quimby, Age 8." Use the graphic organizer to help you.

Practice Book
© Harcourt • Grade 3

Name _____

▲ Read the homophones in parentheses. Complete each sentence with the correct word.

1. (hole, whole)   There is a big __hole__ in my old jeans.

I can't believe I read the __whole__ thing!

2. (flew, flu)   A flock of birds just __flew__ by the window.

Jisela missed school when she had the __flu__.

3. (rains, reins)   When you go horseback riding, hold the __reins__ tightly.

When it __rains__, the hiking trail gets muddy.

4. (meet, meat)   Beef and chicken are two types of __meat__.

I hope I get to __meet__ that movie star.

5. (There, Their)   __There__ are colorful birds on the island.

__Their__ beaks are red and yellow.

6. (write, right)   Caitlyn throws with her __right__ hand.

Beverly is going to __write__ a poem for her mother.

206

Name _____

▲ Complete the riddles by filling in each blank with a word from the box. Then write the word on the second line, dividing it into syllables. Underline the syllable or syllables that make the schwa sound.

sofa	mirror	imitate
cucumber	pizza	reporter

1. A green vegetable with seeds is a __cucumber__

__cu-cum-ber__

2. When you copy what someone says or does, you __imitate__ that person.

__im-i-tate__

3. __Pizza__ is a food made of dough, cheese, tomato sauce, and other toppings.

__piz-za__

4. A __sofa__ is one piece of furniture that might be found in a living room.

__so-fa__

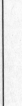

5. A __reporter__ is someone who works for a newspaper.

__re-port-er__

6. A piece of glass that shows your reflection is a __mirror__

__mir-ror__

207

Name _____

▲ Underline the verb in each sentence. Then rewrite the sentence in the tense shown in parentheses ( ).

1. The children study quietly. (past)
   The children studied quietly.

2. The teacher will talk about the report. (past)
   The teacher talked about the report.

3. Many students enjoyed music class. (present)
   Many students enjoy music class.

4. Mr. Green scores the test. (future)
   Mr. Green will score the test.

5. Tim will hurry to school. (present)
   Tim hurries to school.

6. We play outside during recess. (past)
   We played outside during recess.

7. You solved the math problem. (future)
   You will solve the math problem.

8. Misha practices the flute. (past)
   Misha practiced the flute.

School-Home Connection
Work with your child to write three sentences about school. Write one verb in the present tense, one in the past tense, and one in the future tense.

Practice Book
© Harcourt • Grade 3

Name _____

▲ There are four /o͞o/ words spelled with the letters oo and four /o͝o/ words spelled with the letters oo in the word search below. Circle the words. Then write each one in the correct column in the chart.

```
S  R  B  H  M  F  Q  R
P  C  O  O  K  D  J  O
B  R  O  O  K  Z  P  O
E  X  S  D  W  U  W  T
Q  D  T  O  O  T  H  V
C  A  D  R  O  O  P  A
V  P  E  N  L  W  R  D
```

/o͞o/	/o͝o/
boost	hood
root	cook
tooth	brook
droop	wool

School-Home Connection
With the student, think of two more words for each column.

Practice Book
© Harcourt • Grade 3

Left page

Name _____

Theme 5 Review
Lesson 25

▲ Fold the paper along the dotted line. As each spelling word is read aloud, write it in the blank. Then unfold your paper and check your work. Practice writing any spelling words you missed.

Spelling Words

1. choose
2. booth
3. foot
4. bruise
5. threw
6. soft
7. cause
8. thaw
9. false
10. preschool
11. misspell
12. indoors
13. apart
14. across
15. around

1. _____
2. _____
3. _____
4. _____
5. _____
6. _____
7. _____
8. _____
9. _____
10. _____
11. _____
12. _____
13. _____
14. _____
15. _____

210
Practice Book
© Harcourt • Grade 3

Right page

Name _____

Review
Vowel Variant /ô/:
o, au(gh), aw, a(l),
ough
Lesson 25

▲ Circle the word in each sentence that has the /ô/ sound. Then fill in the crossword puzzle with the words.

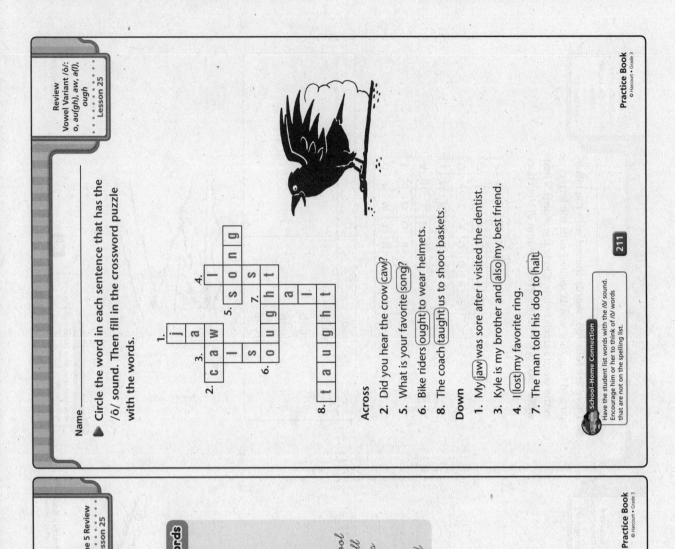

Across

2. Did you hear the crow (caw)?
5. What is your favorite (song)?
6. Bike riders (ought) to wear helmets.
8. The coach (taught) us to shoot baskets.

Down

1. My (jaw) was sore after I visited the dentist.
3. Kyle is my brother and (also) my best friend.
4. I (lost) my favorite ring.
7. The man told his dog to (halt).

School-Home Connection

Have the student list words with the /ô/ sound. Encourage him or her to think of /ô/ words that are not on the spelling list.

211
Practice Book
© Harcourt • Grade 3

© Harcourt • Grade 3

108

Student Edition pp. 210–211

Name _____

▲ Read the story. Then answer the questions about the sequence of events. **Possible responses are shown.**

Spring had come. The snow melted, and flowers began to bloom. The air was warm. In a cozy, hidden cave, a mother bear and her two cubs woke up.

The mother bear went to the cave entrance. She sniffed the air for danger. Then she lumbered outside. Her cubs followed her.

The bears spent all day outside. They ate some berries. After that, they splashed in the cold river. The cubs played with each other while their mother watched.

As night fell, the bears returned to their cave. Their stomachs were full. They were tired and drifted off to sleep.

1. What happens after the mother bear sniffs the air? **She goes outside, and her cubs follow her.**

2. What do the bears do before they splash in the river? **They eat some berries.**

3. What is the last thing the bears do? **They go to sleep in their cave.**

4. What time-order words and phrases are in the story? **Then, all day, after that, while, As night fell, spring,**

School-Home Connection
With the student, think of some other activities the bears might do. Use time-order words and phrases to show when they take place.

Practice Book
© Harcourt • Grade 3

Name _____

▲ Read this part of a student's rough draft. Then answer the questions that follow.

(1) Mia and Simon writing a story. (2) The story are about a robot. (3) The robot is funny. (4) It _____ say all sorts of things. (5) The children are excited. (6) They will show the story to their teacher.

1. Which sentence has a singular subject and the correct form of the verb *be*?
   A Sentence 2
   Ⓑ Sentence 3
   C Sentence 5
   D Sentence 6

2. Which sentence has a plural subject and the correct form of the verb *be*?
   A Sentence 2
   B Sentence 3
   Ⓒ Sentence 5
   D Sentence 6

3. Which sentence has a form of the verb *be* that does NOT agree with the subject?
   Ⓐ Sentence 2
   B Sentence 3
   C Sentence 5
   D Sentence 6

4. Which helping verb should go before the main verb in Sentence 1?
   A have
   B will
   C can
   Ⓓ are

5. Which helping verb could complete Sentence 4?
   A have
   B had
   Ⓒ can
   D is

6. Which other helping verb could replace *will* in Sentence 6?
   A had
   Ⓑ can
   C have
   D were

Practice Book
© Harcourt • Grade 3

Student Edition pp. 212–213

▲ Add *pre-, mis-,* or *in-* to each root word to form a real word. Write the new word on the line.

1. exact ___inexact___

2. heat ___preheat___

3. trust ___mistrust___

4. direct ___indirect___

5. behave ___misbehave___

6. school ___preschool___

7. correct ___incorrect___

8. read ___misread___

9. view ___preview___

10. match ___mismatch___

School-Home Connection
Have the student explain how the prefix changes the meaning of each root word.

▲ Read the article. Circle the letter of the best answer to each question. Then write the author's message.

You are used to getting a letter one or two days after it was mailed. In 1860, though, it could take months for your mail to arrive. That changed when the Pony Express started. It took the Pony Express only ten days to get mail from Missouri to California. Riders on horseback sped across the country with the mail. The riders faced many dangers on the trip, such as rough trails, bad weather, and robberies by bandits. The Pony Express stopped running in 1861 when a telegraph system was built. It connected the entire country. Even though the Pony Express lasted only eighteen months, it was an important way to carry mail across the country.

1. What did the Pony Express carry?

   A ponies

   (B) mail

   C e-mail

2. What was a danger Pony Express riders faced?

   (A) bad weather

   B lack of food

   C closed roads

3. What is the author's message?

Possible response: The Pony Express was an important

way to carry mail across the country.

School-Home Connection
Ask the student to explain which details he or she used to find the author's message.

Name _____

▲ Part A. Read each sentence. Write the Vocabulary Word from the box that is a synonym for the underlined word.

| required | inhabitants | ample |
| functional | amazement | responsibility |

1. The old microwave oven is barely working.

   functional

2. There is enough work to keep everyone busy.

   ample

3. Three eggs are needed for this recipe.

   required

4. My biggest task is to take care of my little sister.

   responsibility

5. The firefighters made sure all the residents of the building got out safely.

   inhabitants

6. Juan jumped up in surprise when he was named the winner.

   amazement

▲ Part B. On a separate sheet of paper, write a sentence describing three *responsibilities* you have at home.

School-Home Connection
Ask the student to list some of the *inhabitants* of the White House.

216 Practice Book
© Harcourt • Grade 3

Name _____

▲ Follow the path from START to FINISH. Shade in the boxes that have a word with the schwa sound. Then answer the questions.

START	about	door	really	calmly	happy	begin
falling	happen	support	nosy	tick	scared	ray
stag	game	alarm	dentist	reckon	carrot	chorus
cast	green	taken	polite	select	gave	FINISH

1. Which words on the path spell the schwa sound with *a*?
   about, alarm

2. Which words on the path spell the schwa sound with *e*?
   happen, taken, select

3. Which words on the path spell the schwa sound with *o*?
   reckon, carrot, polite

4. Which words on the path spell the schwa sound with *u*?
   support, chorus

School-Home Connection
With the student, make up three sentences that each have two of the schwa words.

217 Practice Book
© Harcourt • Grade 3

Name _____

▲ Read this part of a student's rough draft. Then answer the questions that follow.

(1) William loves space. (2) He looked at pictures of the sun and moon when he was younger. (3) Now he read books about the solar system. (4) He will learn about the planets. (5) He will studies space travel. (6) One day he will become an astronaut.

1. Which sentence has a correct past-tense verb?
   A Sentence 1
   B Sentence 2
   C Sentence 4
   D Sentence 5

2. Which sentence has a correct present-tense verb?
   A Sentence 1
   B Sentence 2
   C Sentence 3
   D Sentence 4

3. Which sentence has an incorrect form of a future-tense verb?
   A Sentence 2
   B Sentence 4
   C Sentence 5
   D Sentence 6

4. Which verb should end with an s?
   A looked (Sentence 2)
   B read (Sentence 3)
   C learn (Sentence 4)
   D become (Sentence 6)

5. Which is the future-tense form of the verb in Sentence 1?
   A love
   B will love
   C will loves
   D loved

6. Which is the past-tense form of the verb in Sentence 4?
   A learn
   B learns
   C can learn
   D learned

Practice Book
© Harcourt • Grade 3

Name _____

▲ Read the article below. Write the answer to each question.

Winter is the time when people catch more colds. There are many reasons why people get sick more often in the winter. Children are back in school, sharing germs. The colder weather keeps grown-ups indoors, too. The nearer people are to one another, the more likely they are to spread germs. So what can you do when winter comes? Wash, wash, wash your hands. This gets rid of the germs that get on your hands. If someone is sick, stay away from him or her. And do not share food or drinks.

1. What are two causes of getting sick in the winter?
   Children are back in school, sharing germs. The nearer people are to each other, the more likely they are to spread germs.

2. What is the effect of washing your hands?
   It gets rid of the germs.

3. What are two other ways to avoid getting sick?
   Stay away from sick people. Do not share food or drinks.

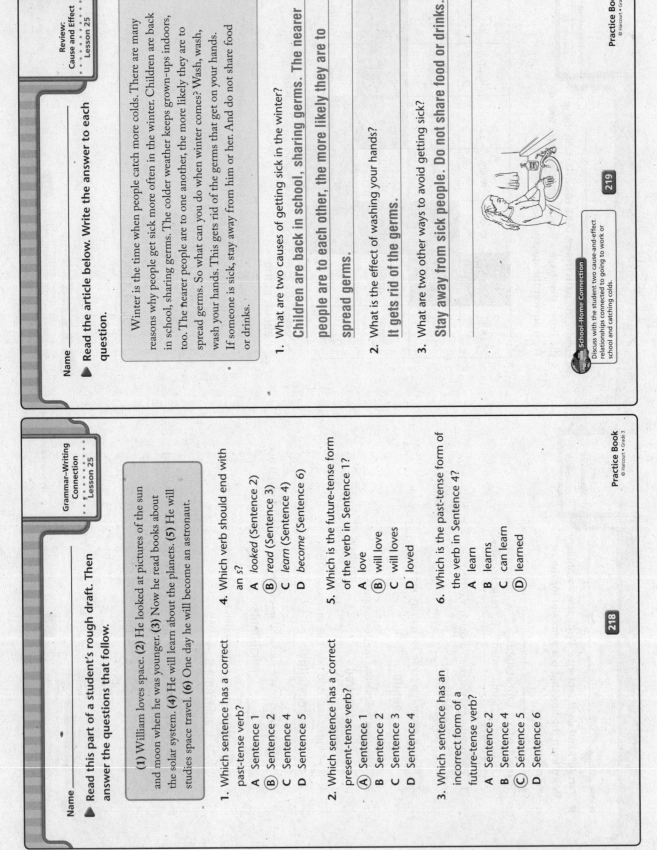

School-Home Connection
Discuss with the student two cause-and-effect relationships connected to going to work or school and catching colds.

219

Practice Book
© Harcourt • Grade 3

Name _____

▲ Read the homophones. Then complete each sentence with the correct word.

1. (pair, pear)   I wore my favorite __pair__ of jeans today.

The __pear__ was ripe.

2. (be, bee)   The buzzing __bee__ landed near Jane.

I hope I will __be__ fast enough to win the race.

3. (feat, feet)   Tonya's __feet__ were sore after the hike.

The acrobat performed an amazing __feat__ of strength.

4. (horse, hoarse)   Shouting so loudly made me __hoarse__.

Kari rode her __horse__ every afternoon.

5. (beat, beet)   I had a __beet__ salad for lunch.

Our team __beat__ theirs in the final game.

6. (peak, peek)   Wait until we get to the mountain __peak__.

Did you __peek__ at your present?

Spelling Words

1. section
2. caution
3. fiction
4. nation
5. action
6. vision
7. vacation
8. motion
9. question
10. mention
11. station
12. attention
13. portion
14. collection
15. session

Name _____

▲ Read the Spelling Words. Sort the words and write them where they belong. **Order may vary.**

Words with -tion

1. section
2. caution
3. fiction
4. nation
5. action
6. vacation
7. motion
8. question
9. mention
10. station
11. attention
12. portion
13. collection

Words with -sion

14. vision
15. session

▲ Read the story. Then answer the questions.

Leslie's father owns a music store. It is filled with all kinds of instruments that he sells and repairs.

Leslie helps at the music shop after school, keeping the violins, flutes, and trumpets shiny and clean. "Hi, Dad, how's business?" she asked as she arrived one afternoon.

"Well, we just received some beautiful, new guitars. They're really expensive ones. I put the cases over by the wall," he replied.

"Oh!" Leslie exclaimed as she saw them. "They *are* beautiful. Can I try one?"

Her father hesitated. "Well, what about your homework? Maybe you should do that," he said, taking a glance at the guitars.

"I don't have any homework today," said Leslie. "Can I try one?"

"Well, maybe you should help with something else—like that flute over there. Perhaps that would be better," he said slowly.

"But I *always* polish the flutes. Why can't I help with the new guitars?" she asked.

"Well," said her dad. "Why don't we try one of the guitars together. Will that make you happy?"

"Yes! Don't worry. I remember how to hold a guitar," she said.

1. What does Leslie's dad say about the guitars?
   "Well, we just received some expensive new guitars."

2. Why does Leslie's Dad mention her homework?
   He is nervous about her handling the guitars.

3. Why does Leslie's father not want her to try a guitar?
   Possible response: They are very expensive and he is afraid she might damage one.

School–Home Connection
Help the student suggest another reason why Leslie's dad might not want her to try a guitar.

222

Practice Book
© Harcourt • Grade 3

▲ Complete each sentence. Combine a root from the box with *-tion* or *-sion* to make the missing word.

| quest | inject | object |
| collect | affect | act |

1. It is important to take _____ action _____ to help protect manatees.

2. Do you have any _____ objection _____ to riding in the back seat of a car?

3. He has a small _____ collection _____ of sea shells.

4. A hug is a form of _____ affection _____.

5. Dr. Harris gave the patient an _____ injection _____.

6. Do you have a _____ question _____ for the guest speaker?

School–Home Connection
Have the student write sentences with the following words: session, affection, and admission.

223

Practice Book
© Harcourt • Grade 3

Name _____

▲ Complete the sentence about each Vocabulary Word.

1. If someone is _____, he or she is a **nuisance**.

   Possible response: talking too loudly _____

2. Someone who _____ is **boasting**.

   Possible response: congratulates himself _____

3. Trees move _____ when they **sway**.

   Possible response: back and forth _____

4. If you **oblige** someone, you make them feel as if you _____.

   Possible response: have done something nice for them _____

5. If you are **summoning** someone, you are _____.

   Possible response: trying to get that person's attention. _____

6. If a dog is **sedentary**, it _____.

   Possible response: does not move very much. _____

School–Home Connection

Have the student think of different things he or she can do to *oblige* a family member and make a list of these things.

Practice Book
© Harcourt • Grade 3

224

Name _____

▲ As you read "Charlotte's Web," fill in the graphic organizer. Then answer the questions below.

Characters	Setting
Wilbur	

Plot

1. Who are some characters in the story?

   Possible response: Wilbur, Fern, Charlotte, Templeton _____

2. What is the setting of the story?

   Possible response: a barnyard _____

▲ On a separate sheet of paper, summarize the selection. Use the graphic organizer to help you.

Multiple-Meaning Words
Lesson 26

▲ Read each sentence. Look at the word in dark print. Then write a new sentence with this word but using a *different* meaning.

1. I can jump three feet in the air!
Possible response: My *feet* are growing so fast, I need new shoes!

2. Do you have a **match** for the campfire?
Possible response: Peanut butter and jelly is a good *match.*

3. The living room has only one **coat** of paint.
Possible response: My new winter *coat* is 100% wool.

4. The math and science **clubs** sponsor the annual science competition.
Possible response: My dad just bought new golf *clubs.*

5. The **change** in weather is annoying.
Possible response: The clerk counted out my *change.*

6. A hand **wave** means "hello."
Possible response: The enormous ocean *wave* knocked down the surfers.

School-Home Connection
Help the student pick three words and come up with a list of descriptive phrases for each one. For example: *muddy feet, wooden club, or a friendly wave.*

Practice Book
© Harcourt • Grade 3

Review Suffixes -tion and -sion
Lesson 26

▲ Complete each sentence with a word from the Word Box.

profession	action	reaction	collection	question
decision	correction	attention	tension	vision

1. Raul's father's **profession** _____ is law.

2. I always pay **attention** _____ in class.

3. I made a **decision** _____ to go to Mia's party.

4. There was lots of **action** _____ in the championship game.

5. The class felt a great deal of **tension** _____ before the test.

6. Trey has a huge stamp **collection** _____.

7. I need to make a **correction** _____ to that story.

8. Nora's face showed her **reaction** _____ to the news.

9. Shirley has a **question** _____ about turtles.

10. Ernastein learned that opossums have poor **vision** _____ and hearing, but can smell very well.

School-Home Connection
Help the student use the words *tension, action, and collection* in a short, funny story about a contest of some kind.

Practice Book
© Harcourt • Grade 3

Lesson 26 — Irregular Verbs

Name _____

▲ Rewrite each sentence, using the verb tense in parentheses ( ).

1. The spider laid eggs. (present tense)
   The spider lays eggs.

2. I have two books on spiders. (past tense)
   I had two books on spiders.

3. The farmer's daughter had done her chores. (present tense)
   The farmer's daughter does her chores.

4. She sits at the kitchen table. (past tense)
   She sat at the kitchen table.

5. Her brother comes home from school. (past tense)
   Her brother came home from school.

6. He will say "giddyup" to the horse. (past tense)
   He said "giddyup" to the horse.

7. The neighbors raised their new flag. (present tense)
   The neighbors raise their new flag.

8. We saw many animals on the farm. (present tense)
   We see many animals on the farm.

School-Home Connection
Ask your child to choose an irregular verb from this lesson. Then work with him or her to write three sentences, using the verb in a different tense each time.

228 Practice Book
© Harcourt • Grade 3

V/V Syllable Pattern — Lesson 27

Name _____

Spelling Words
1. lion
2. dial
3. idea
4. neon
5. science
6. area
7. radio
8. quiet
9. piano
10. fluid
11. video
12. loyal
13. stereo
14. pliers
15. create

▲ Read the Spelling Words. Sort the words and write them where they belong.

Words with Two Vowel Sounds in the Middle

1. lion
2. dial
3. neon
4. quiet
5. piano
6. loyal
7. create
8. fluid
9. pliers
10. science

Words with Two Vowel Sounds at the End

11. radio
12. video
13. idea
14. area
15. stereo

School-Home Connection
Ask your child why he or she wrote the Spelling Words in each part of the chart. Discuss other words that follow the same syllable patterns.

229 Practice Book
© Harcourt • Grade 3

Student Edition pp. 228–229

Name _____

▲ Read the following story. Then circle the letter of the best answer to each question.

Long ago in China, there were two sisters who were weavers of silk. One day a lady, followed by her many servants, came to their shop. "I want a gown," she said. "You will each make twenty yards of your best silk. Then I will choose which I want. I will come for it in two days."

The sisters, Siwo and Sun, went to work. For two days they spun silk. Again and again Sun bragged, "I am a much better worker than you!" Siwo only replied. "One must work carefully to make silk."

In two days, the lady returned. As she looked at Siwo's silk, Siwo apologized, "I could only make fifteen yards of silk."

"Lady," Sun interrupted, "I have made twenty-five yards of silk!" The lady looked at Sun's silk. "Siwo's silk will make the prettiest gown."

1. Which words from the story suggest that the lady is rich and important?
   A The sisters, Siwo and Sun, went to work.
   B "One must work carefully to make silk."
   Ⓒ followed by her many servants

2. Which words from the story suggest that Sun is vain?
   Ⓐ Again and again Sun bragged
   B "Siwo's silk will make the prettiest gown."
   C The lady looked at Sun's silk.

3. Which words from the story suggest that Siwo had made the best silk?
   A "I want a gown."
   B In two days, the lady returned.
   Ⓒ "Siwo's silk will make the prettiest gown."

School-Home Connection
Have the student write two facts from the story. Then help him or her make an inference based on those two facts.

Practice Book
© Harcourt • Grade 3

230

Name _____

▲ Write each word from the box next to a word that rhymes with it. If the word has two syllables, draw a line to show where the syllables divide.

| feud | react | fuel | lead |
| loud | reuse | road | sour |

1. rude ____ feud

2. mode ____ road

3. excuse ____ re/use

4. seed ____ lead

5. attract ____ re/act

6. jewel ____ fu/el

7. crowd ____ loud

8. power ____ sou/r

School-Home Connection
Have the student write two-syllable words that rhyme with higher. Then have him or her divide those words into syllables.

Practice Book
© Harcourt • Grade 3

231

118

© Harcourt • Grade 3

Student Edition pp. 230–231

Name _____

▲ Write the letter of the Vocabulary Word that best matches each definition.

A spiral

B social

C reels

D prey

E shallow

F strands

__D__ 1. an animal that is hunted for food

__A__ 2. a shape that curls around and around in a circle

__F__ 3. long pieces of something

__B__ 4. living in groups of similar animals

__C__ 5. to wind something in

__E__ 6. not very deep

Name _____

▲ Use the graphic organizer to record facts from "Spiders and Their Webs." Fill in the box on the left with things you already know about spiders. In the box on the right, write what you learn as you read. Make inferences in the bottom box. Possible responses are shown.

What You Know

Insects can cause disease.

You cannot avoid what you cannot see.

Individuals who like to be around people are social.

What the Author Tells You

Spiders capture insects.

Golden orb weavers spin gold webs in sunny places.

Thousands of social spiders work together in groups.

Inferences

Spiders help control disease.

Golden orb weavers spin gold webs in sunny places to make them harder to see.

Social spiders got their name because they work together in groups.

▲ On a separate sheet of paper, summarize the selection with three of your inferences. Use the graphic organizer to help you.

Name _____

▲ Read the meanings in the box below. In each
sentence, which meaning of the underlined word
is used? Write the letter of the correct meaning on the line.

A to deal with something in a court of law
B to attempt
C to make demands on something
D a piece of metal that holds things in place
E what happens when you grab and hold something
F the amount of fish captured
G a flaw or mistake

1. Please try to do your best in the game. __B__

2. The judge will try the case tomorrow. __A__

3. Sometimes my little brother can try my patience! __C__

4. The center fielder made an amazing catch. __E__

5. Mia's catch set a record for most trout in a day. __F__

6. There was only one catch in our plan. __G__

7. The catch on the zipper broke off. __D__

School-Home Connection
Have the student use a dictionary to find at
least two meanings for the word *leave*.

234

Practice Book
© Harcourt • Grade 3

Name _____

▲ Use the words in the box to complete the
sentences. Then divide those words into syllables.

| appreciate | poetry | idea | biology |
| dial | science | violin | pliers |

1. Will you __d i / a l__ the telephone number for me?

2. Let's think of a better __i / d e / a__.

3. Remove the nail with the __p l i / e r s__.

4. The poet writes lovely __p o e t / r y__.

5. We learned about frogs in __s c i / e n c e__ class.

6. Two kinds of science are chemistry and __b i / o l / o g / y__.

7. She started taking __v i / o / l i n__ lessons
when she was five years old.

8. I __a p / p r e c i / a t e__
that you came for a visit.

School-Home Connection
Have the student write a sentence that
includes one V/V word. Then have him or her
divide that word into syllables.

235

Practice Book
© Harcourt • Grade 3

Name _____

Adverbs
Lesson 27

▲ Write the adverb in each sentence. Then write the verb that it describes.

1. My teacher talks excitedly about science.

   excitedly, talks

2. Tomorrow we will learn about insects.

   Tomorrow, learn (will learn)

3. Of all the students, Evan studied the longest.

   the longest, studied

4. I speak more softly than the other students at the library.

   more softly, speak

▲ Rewrite each sentence. Complete it with an adverb that answers the question in parentheses ( ).
Possible responses are shown.

5. This spider crawls _____ than that spider. (How?)

   This spider crawls more quickly than that spider.

6. I put my report _____. (Where?)

   I put my report there.

7. _____ you will learn about the sun. (When?)

   Now you will learn about the sun.

Name _____

Suffixes
-able, -ible,
-less, -ous
Lesson 28

▲ Read the Spelling Words. Sort the words and write them where they belong.

Spelling Words

1. doable
2. famous
3. careless
4. various
5. endless
6. reliable
7. nervous
8. useless
9. flexible
10. washable
11. helpless
12. terrible
13. valuable
14. dangerous
15. powerless

Words with -able

1. doable
2. reliable
3. washable
4. valuable

Words with -ible

5. flexible
6. terrible

Words with -less

7. careless
8. endless
9. useless
10. helpless
11. powerless

Words with -ous

12. famous   14. nervous
13. various   15. dangerous

Suffixes:
-able, -ible
Lesson 28

▶ Complete the story by adding *-able* or *-ible* to each unfinished word.

It was Aunt Marta's birthday, and Celia wanted to give her the best birthday party poss __ible__. She baked a cake and invited all of Aunt Marta's friends and family. Then she put on some suit __able__ clothes.

As she was dressing, though, Marta heard a terr __ible__ racket. When she looked out the window, she saw her three little brothers playing instruments. They were very aud __ible__, even through the window. But the music they made was laugh __able__! It sounded more like a lot of banging and screeching than actual music. Still, Marta thought, her brothers might be train __able__.

For the next hour, Marta helped her little brothers learn a song. They practiced hard. "Who says little kids are not teach __able__?" she said to herself over and over again.

Later, at Aunt Marta's birthday dinner, the three brothers played "Happy Birthday" for Aunt Marta and all of the guests.

"Wow," everyone said when it was over. "This celebration is incred __ible__!"

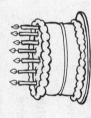

Practice Book
© Harcourt • Grade 3

School-Home Connection
Have the student make up a new sentence for each completed word. (For example: *It is not possible for me to fly through the air like a bird.*)

Make Predictions
Lesson 28

▶ Read the story. Then answer the questions.

"But it's vacation!" cried Nick. "I don't want to go visit Uncle James!"

"You've never even met him," Dad said. "He's a very interesting person."

Two weeks later, Nick and his father were staring at Uncle James's big old house in the country. "His house looks creepy," grumbled Nick.

Dad only smiled. "Uncle James has some unusual things. He might even show you his special trunk!"

"Who cares about an old trunk," Nick muttered.

Suddenly, a very small, elderly man opened the door. "So this must be Nick," said Uncle James. "You look just like your Uncle Phil. He was a famous mountain climber. He climbed every tall peak in North America."

"Wow," said Nick. He was impressed that he had a famous relative.

After dinner, Uncle James opened up an old trunk. In it were pictures, letters, and even newspaper articles. One by one, Uncle James introduced Nick to relatives from long ago. There were cowhands, sea captains, and even his Aunt Emma, who had lived to be 106.

1. What does Nick say about Uncle James in the beginning of the story?

"I don't want to go visit Uncle James!"

2. What is your prediction for what will happen next?

Possible response: Nick will want to learn more about his
family; Nick will enjoy his time with Uncle James.

3. Which story clue helped you make a prediction?

Possible response: Nick was impressed to learn he had
a famous relative; he sat while Uncle James shared the
contents of the trunk.

Practice Book
© Harcourt • Grade 3

School-Home Connection
Have the student tell you an ending that will be appropriate for the story.

Name _____

Robust Vocabulary
Lesson 28

▲ Circle the word that correctly completes each sentence.

1. The chef _____ pepper on the salad.

    expand   (sprinkled)   erupt

2. The scientist did careful and _____ research on volcanoes.

    grainy   (thorough)   deliberation

3. The soup looked _____ and lumpy.

    erupt   sprinkled   (grainy)

4. The team will _____ if more people join.

    (expand)   deliberation   thorough

5. The jury reached its decision after a long _____.

    sprinkled   thorough   (deliberation)

6. That volcano may _____ soon.

    thorough   grainy   (erupt)

Name _____

Reader's Guide
Lesson 28

▲ Realistic fiction has details that help you make predictions about events to come. You can read ahead to revise or confirm your predictions. **Possible responses are shown.**

Beginning

Prediction: **Beany will be nervous at the science fair.**

Look at the pictures and read pages 358–359. Use details to make a prediction about what will happen next.

→

Middle

Confirm/Revise Prediction: **Beany was nervous at the science fair.**

New Prediction: **Beany and Kevin will win first place.**

Look at the pictures and read pages 361–368. Confirm your prediction.

→

End

Confirm/Revise Prediction: **Beany and Kevin won first place.**

Look at the pictures and read pages 369–370. Revise or confirm your prediction. Make a new prediction about what will happen next.

▲ On a separate sheet of paper, write a summary of "The Science Fair."

Name _____

▲ Read each homograph and its two pronunciations.
Write the letter of the pronunciation that goes
with each sentence.

close	a. klōs	b. klōz	tear	c. ter	d. tir
lead	e. led	f. lēd	does	g. duz	h. dōz
wind	i. wind	j. wīnd

1. The **wind** blew the papers down the street. __i__

2. Please do not **tear** my paper. __c__

3. The mother hen will **lead** her chicks to the pond. __f__

4. Two **does** and two fawns drank from the river. __h__

5. Did you remember to **close** the door? __b__

6. I felt sad, and a **tear** came to my eye. __d__

7. Frida has to **wind** her alarm clock every evening. __j__

8. **Does** anyone know where my pencil is? __g__

9. A kite made of **lead** will never fly. __e__

10. My friend lives very **close** to me. __a__

School-Home Connection
Have the student state the definition of a
homograph in his or her own words.

242

© Harcourt • Grade 3

Practice Book
© Harcourt • Grade 3

Name _____

▲ Each underlined word has the wrong suffix.
Rewrite the words with the correct suffixes.
Use -able, -ible, -less or -ous.

1. The clothes that I bought today are wash<u>less</u>.
   __washable__

2. Is that paintbrush still us<u>ous</u>?
   __usable__

3. Those circus acrobats are flex<u>ous</u>!
   __flexible__

4. The movie was so long it seemed end<u>ible</u>.
   __endless__

5. If you are rely<u>ous</u>, I will let you borrow this CD.
   __reliable__

6. Try not to be so nerve<u>able</u> when you perform.
   __nervous__

7. It is too danger<u>able</u> to ride your bike down that hill.
   __dangerous__

8. Mona was bored and rest<u>able</u>.
   __restless__

School-Home Connection
Have the student give an oral definition for
each word he or she wrote.

243

Practice Book
© Harcourt • Grade 3

Contractions
Lesson 28

Name _____

▲ Rewrite each sentence. Replace each contraction with the words used to form it.

1. Alice doesn't see that we're waving.
   Alice does not see that we are waving.

2. She's worried that we haven't arrived.
   She is worried that we have not arrived.

3. I'm glad that you didn't stay home.
   I am glad that you did not stay home.

4. It isn't clear that he's the winner.
   It is not clear that he is the winner.

▲ If the sentence is correct, write correct. If it is not, rewrite it correctly.   A possible response is shown.

5. Wouldn't you like any help?
   correct

6. I don't see my teacher nowhere.
   I don't see my teacher anywhere.

7. There wasn't nobody in the cafeteria.
   There wasn't anybody in the cafeteria.

Practice Book
© Harcourt • Grade 3

School-Home Connection
Work with your child to write three sentences about his or her day, using contractions. Use at least one contraction with a pronoun and one with not.

Prefixes
bi-, non-, over-
Lesson 29

Name _____

▲ Read the Spelling Words. Sort the words and write them where they belong.

Spelling Words
1. overnight
2. bicycle
3. nonstop
4. overdue
5. overlook
6. biweekly
7. overflow
8. nonsense
9. oversee
10. overhead
11. nonfiction
12. overcoat
13. nonfat
14. overdone
15. biplane

Words with bi-

1. bicycle
2. biweekly
3. biplane

Words with non-

4. nonstop
5. nonsense
6. nonfiction
7. nonfat

Words with over-

8. overnight
9. overdue
10. overlook
11. overflow
12. oversee
13. overhead
14. overcoat
15. overdone

Practice Book
© Harcourt • Grade 3

School-Home Connection
With your child, write sentences using each Spelling Word. Discuss how the prefixes bi-, non-, and over- change the meaning of each base word.

Student Edition pp. 244–245

▲ **Read the story. Then answer each question about it.** Possible responses are shown.

Vanessa and Keisha were walking home through the park. They were busy chatting, and they paid no attention to where they were. Just beyond the swings, there was a soccer field. Suddenly a strange-looking object landed right in the middle of it. It made no sound, and the girls were too busy to notice anyway. They just kept walking and talking. Then, just as they were almost past the strange object, voices began to come from it. "Do you hear something?" Vanessa asked.

1. What will happen next?
The girls will stop and look at the strange-looking object

in the park.

2. What story clues helped you make your prediction?
A UFO-type vehicle is very unusual to see in a park, so

once the girls notice it, they probably will want to know

what it is.

3. What do you know from your experience that helped you make your prediction?
Young people are curious and might not be afraid to look

into something unusual.

School–Home Connection

Read the story with the student. Then work together to write an ending. Be sure to point out story clues that helped you make your predictions.

246

Practice Book
© Harcourt • Grade 3

▲ **Write a word from the box to complete each sentence.**

overcoat	biweekly	nonstop	overflow
nonfiction	overnight	biplane	bicycle

1. My little brother runs around _____ nonstop _____.

2. The old _____ biplane _____ flies very slowly.

3. The _____ overcoat _____ she wore over her dress was long

and very warm.

4. Gia prefers fiction to _____ nonfiction _____.

5. We will stay _____ overnight _____ at the campground.

6. That magazine comes out _____ biweekly _____, or every

two weeks.

7. The river began to _____ overflow _____ its banks.

8. Tara's _____ bicycle _____ has narrow tires.

School–Home Connection

Ask the student to explain how he or she knew which word to use in each sentence.

247

Practice Book
© Harcourt • Grade 3

Name _____

▲ Use a Vocabulary Word to complete each
sentence.

| rotates | steady | reflects |
| surface | evidence | appears |

1. We see the moon at night because it __reflects__ light from
the sun.

2. All the __evidence__ suggested that he had not discovered a
new planet.

3. When you spin the classroom globe, it __rotates__ around
and around.

4. My mom held the ladder __steady__ so Aunt Nita could
paint the ceiling.

5. That little dog __appears__ to be frightened by the storm.

6. The __surface__ of that table is smooth.

Name _____

▲ Use the graphic organizer to record what you
already know about the planets. Put this information
under *What I Know*. Then ask questions for what you
want to know about the planets. Put the questions
under *What I Want to Know*. After reading, write what
you have learned from "The Planets" under *What I Learned*.
Possible responses are shown.

What I Know	What I Want to Know	What I Learned
In the sky, there are planets, stars, a sun, and a moon.	How is a planet different from a star?	A planet is seen because the sun shines on it. A star gives off its own light.
We live on Earth.	How do planets move and rotate?	Planets orbit the sun.
Each planet has different features.	What are some features of each planet?	Mercury—hot and cold; Venus—rotates opposite direction; Earth—has life; Mars—once had water; Jupiter—gases form Great Red Spot; Saturn—hundreds of rings; Uranus—long orbit; Neptune—looks blue; Pluto—cold and small.

▲ On a separate sheet of paper, summarize the selection, providing
facts you have learned about the planets. Use the graphic organizer
to help you. **Answers will vary.**

Homographs
Lesson 29

▲ Read each sentence. Then draw a line to match
the underlined homograph with the correct
definition.

1. A gray dove sat in the tree.

   the past tense of dive

   a type of bird

2. Tim sings bass in our chorus.

   a type of fish

   a voice with a deep sound

3. My sister will polish her trumpet.

   to shine

   relating to the country
   of Poland

4. We will present a gift to our teacher.

   to give in a formal way

   a gift

5. Temperatures were very hot out
   on the sandy desert.

   a land area without water

   to flee or run away

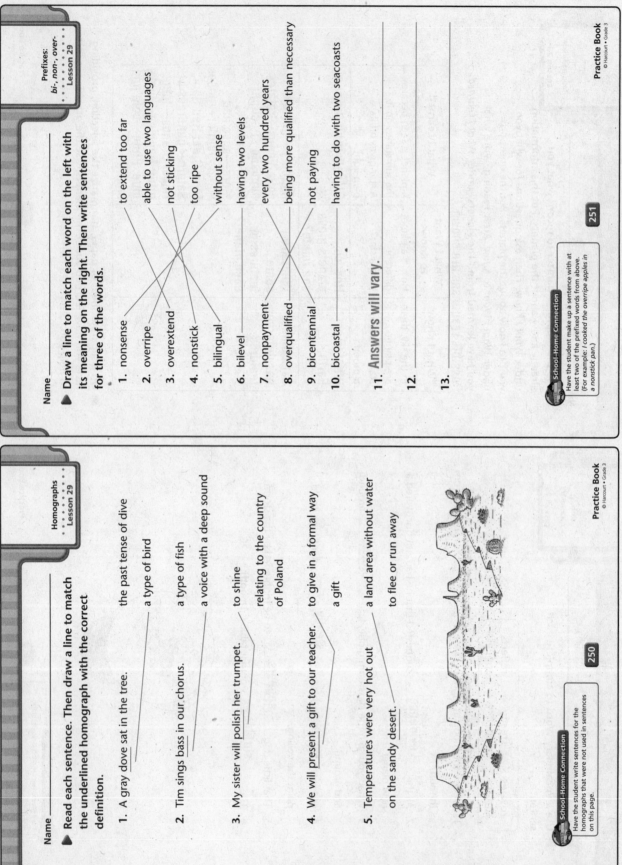

250

Prefixes:
bi-, non-, over-
Lesson 29

▲ Draw a line to match each word on the left with
its meaning on the right. Then write sentences
for three of the words.

1. nonsense   to extend too far

2. overripe   able to use two languages

3. overextend   not sticking

4. nonstick   too ripe

5. bilingual   without sense

6. bilevel   having two levels

7. nonpayment   every two hundred years

8. overqualified   being more qualified than necessary

9. bicentennial   not paying

10. bicoastal   having to do with two seacoasts

11. _Answers will vary._ _____

12. _____

13. _____

251

Name

▲ **Rewrite each sentence correctly.**

1. sometimes i sing my favorite song.

   Sometimes I sing my favorite song.

2. that song is called twinkle, twinkle, little star.

   That song is called "Twinkle, Twinkle, Little Star."

3. those three stars are named altair castor and polaris.

   Those three stars are named Altair, Castor, and Polaris.

4. sirius is the brightest star in the sky and i see it at night.

   Sirius is the brightest star in the sky, and I see it at night.

5. you can read about stars in a magazine called Ask.

   You can read about stars in a magazine called Ask.

6. mrs. wong reads to children at the library in middletown.

   Mrs. Wong reads to children at the library in Middletown.

7. she lives in new york but she works in connecticut.

   She lives in New York, but she works in Connecticut.

8. today she reads the book a child's introduction to the night sky.

   Today she reads the book A Child's Introduction to the Night Sky.

252

Name

▲ **Part A. Add -tion or -sion to the following root words.**

1. omit   **omission**

2. infect   **infection**

3. explode   **explosion**

4. celebrate   **celebration**

5. decide   **decision**

▲ **Part B. Use the words you wrote in Part A to complete the following sentences.**

6. When the fireworks went off, they made a loud **explosion** .

7. Choosing a present for someone can be a difficult **decision** .

8. We had a **celebration** for my sister's high school graduation.

9. Emily is at home with an ear **infection** .

10. The **omission** of two letters on the sign made it very confusing!

253

▲ Fold the paper along the dotted line. As each
spelling word is read aloud, write it in the blank.
Then unfold your paper, and check your work.
Practice writing any spelling words you missed.

Spelling Words

1. vision
2. caution
3. session
4. fluid
5. piano
6. loyal
7. reliable
8. flexible
9. powerless
10. dangerous
11. famous
12. biplane
13. nonstop
14. overnight
15. oversee

1. _____
2. _____
3. _____
4. _____
5. _____
6. _____
7. _____
8. _____
9. _____
10. _____
11. _____
12. _____
13. _____
14. _____
15. _____

▲ Look at each row of words. Underline the word
that has the V/V syllable pattern. Then use it in
a sentence on the line below. Divide the V/V word
into syllables.

1. l a i d o u t f u e l

Possible response: We put fu/el in our car on Friday.

2. l o u d s c i e n c e f l i e s

Possible response: Sci/ence is my favorite subject.

3. r e a c t r o a d d o e s

Possible response: He did not re/act to the loud noise.

4. l i e s t r i e d c e r e a l m e a t

Possible response: Pedro ate ce/re/al for breakfast.

5. d i a r y d a i r y l e a d

Possible response: Li writes in her di/a/ry every night.

School-Home Connection

For each word, have the student write another
word in which the same letters make the same
V/V sound.

Name _____

Review: Make Inferences
Lesson 30

▲ Read the story. Then write your answers to the questions on the lines below.

Aida dropped her bag and sat down. Her face was bright red, and she wiped the sweat off her forehead.

"Aida, what's wrong?" asked her brother Tim.

Aida poured a glass of water and drank it all. "Coach Lee made us do four extra laps!"

Tim dropped a few ice cubes into Aida's glass. "Sounds like the new coach is really tough on the team."

"We're getting ready for the big game next week," Aida replied. She leaned her head back and closed her eyes.

"Are you nervous?" asked Tim.

"No, not yet," said Aida.

1. How do you think Aida feels? How can you tell?

Possible response: She feels tired. She is sweaty, sits

down, leans her head back, and closes her eyes; exercise

always makes me tired.

2. How do you think Tim feels about Aida?

Possible response: Tim likes Aida because he puts ice

cubes in her glass and asks how she feels.

3. How do you think Aida will feel on the day of her big game? Why?

Possible response: Nervous. She says that she is not

nervous yet, which means that she expects to be nervous

later. I usually feel nervous before big games.

School-Home Connection

Have the student tell you the facts that helped him or her answer these questions. For example, Aida is tired because she is sweating.

256

Name _____

Grammar–Writing
Connection
Lesson 30

▲ Read this part of a student's rough draft. Then answer the questions that follow.

(1) Yesterday my class went to an animal park. (2) We saw lions from the window of the school bus. (3) One lion _____ on a rock. (4) Monkeys played happily in the trees. (5) Some of them come excitedly to the bus. (6) _____, I will write a story about all the animals I seen.

1. Which of these verb forms could go in the blank in Sentence 3?

    A sit
    B sets
    C sat
    D set

2. Which verb needs the helping verb *have* before it?

    A went (Sentence 1)
    B saw (Sentence 2)
    C write (Sentence 6)
    D seen (Sentence 6)

3. Which is the past-tense form that could replace the underlined verb in Sentence 5?

    A comes
    B comed
    C came
    D camed

4. Which sentence has an adverb that tells *when*?

    A Sentence 1
    B Sentence 2
    C Sentence 4
    D Sentence 5

5. Which sentence does NOT have an adverb?

    A Sentence 1
    B Sentence 2
    C Sentence 4
    D Sentence 5

6. Which adverb could go in the blank in Sentence 6?

    A Tomorrow
    B More quickly
    C Most slowly
    D More slow

257

Review: Prefixes:
bi-, non-, over-
Lesson 30

▲ Underline the word with a prefix in each
sentence. Then write its meaning on the line.
Possible responses are shown.

1. Our <u>bicoastal</u> flight from New York to California took five and a

    half hours.
    having to do with two coasts

2. Billy took all <u>nonessential</u> items out of his backpack.
    not essential

3. None of the <u>overhead</u> lights was on when we got home.
    above the head

4. Mareeka made a face when she took a bite of the <u>overripe</u> banana.
    more than ripe

5. What Trina said was <u>nonsense</u>, so we did not believe her.
    words that do not make sense

6. The <u>bilevel</u> house is the biggest on our street.
    having two levels

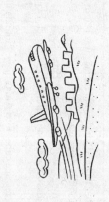

School-Home Connection
Have the student explain the meaning of each
word with a prefix.

258

Practice Book
© Harcourt • Grade 3

Review:
Multiple-Meaning
Words
Lesson 30

▲ Read each sentence. Then choose the sentence
that uses the same meaning for the underlined
word. Circle the letter of the best answer.

1. Please <u>lay</u> those bags down carefully.
    A Chickens can lay more than three hundred eggs per year.
    (B) John will lay his clothes out on his bed.

2. Whom did you <u>pick</u> to play on your kickball team?
    (A) Mom let me pick what we had for dinner last night.
    B We will pick flowers from our garden to put on the table.

3. It is hard to <u>tie</u> a butterfly knot.
    (A) Do not forget to tie your shoes before you leave.
    B Gina scored a basket to tie the game.

4. I used <u>tape</u> to fix my torn paper.
    A Please put the tape in the VCR.
    (B) Herman attached the picture to the wall with tape.

5. The leaves change color in the <u>fall</u>.
    A The ice skater's fall looked painful.
    (B) Do you prefer fall or winter?

6. Dan took a <u>trip</u> to the park.
    (A) I would like to go on a hiking trip.
    B A trip over loose wires can cause a sprained ankle.

School-Home Connection
Ask the student to write a sentence that uses
the second meaning of *fall* from #5.

259

Practice Book
© Harcourt • Grade 3

Name _____

▲ Part A. Draw a line to match each Vocabulary Word with its definition.

1. observed
2. confirm
3. magnify
4. picturesque
5. generates
6. safeguard

a. to keep safe
b. to make bigger
c. creates or makes
d. to make sure
e. looked at closely
f. like a picture

▲ Part B. Write answers to the questions on the lines below.

7. What are three ways you could confirm that it was snowing outside?

Possible responses: watch the weather report, look out the window, go outside

8. If you observed a bird's nest for a day, what might you see?

Possible response: I might see a mother bird feeding her babies, or I might see eggs hatching.

School-Home Connection
Ask the student to name a place where he or she might find a machine that generates snow.

Name _____

▲ Use the clues to complete the puzzle. Use words with suffixes.

ACROSS
1. capable of being relied upon
4. capable of being reached
7. full of fame
8. without power

DOWN
2. without end
3. capable of being worn
5. full of humor
6. capable of being done

School-Home Connection
Have the student think of one more word for each suffix.

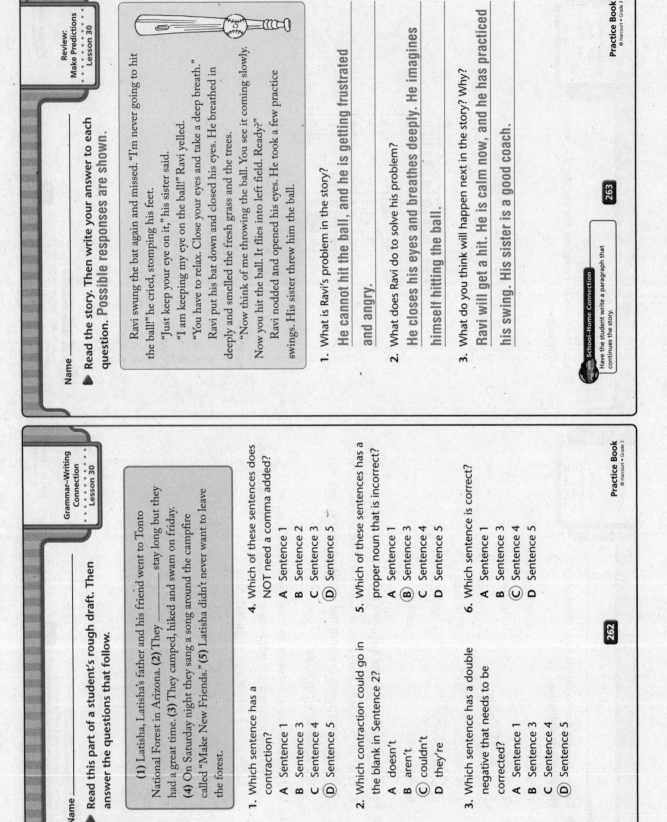

Left page (Student Edition p. 262)

▲ Read this part of a student's rough draft. Then answer the questions that follow.

(1) Latisha, Latisha's father and his friend went to Tonto National Forest in Arizona. (2) They _____ stay long but they had a great time. (3) They camped, hiked and swam on friday. (4) On Saturday night they sang a song around the campfire called "Make New Friends." (5) Latisha didn't never want to leave the forest.

1. Which sentence has a contraction?
   A Sentence 1
   B Sentence 3
   C Sentence 4
   D Sentence 5

2. Which contraction could go in the blank in Sentence 2?
   A doesn't
   B aren't
   C couldn't
   D they're

3. Which sentence has a double negative that needs to be corrected?
   A Sentence 1
   B Sentence 3
   C Sentence 4
   D Sentence 5

4. Which of these sentences does NOT need a comma added?
   A Sentence 1
   B Sentence 2
   C Sentence 3
   D Sentence 5

5. Which of these sentences has a proper noun that is incorrect?
   A Sentence 1
   B Sentence 3
   C Sentence 4
   D Sentence 5

6. Which sentence is correct?
   A Sentence 1
   B Sentence 3
   C Sentence 4
   D Sentence 5

Right page (Student Edition p. 263)

▲ Read the story. Then write your answer to each question. Possible responses are shown.

Ravi swung the bat again and missed. "I'm never going to hit the ball!" he cried, stomping his feet.

"Just keep your eye on it," his sister said.

"I am keeping my eye on the ball!" Ravi yelled.

"You have to relax. Close your eyes and take a deep breath." Ravi put his bat down and closed his eyes. He breathed in deeply and smelled the fresh grass and the trees.

"Now think of me throwing the ball. You see it coming slowly. Now you hit the ball. It flies into left field. Ready?"

Ravi nodded and opened his eyes. He took a few practice swings. His sister threw him the ball.

1. What is Ravi's problem in the story?
   He cannot hit the ball, and he is getting frustrated
   and angry.

2. What does Ravi do to solve his problem?
   He closes his eyes and breathes deeply. He imagines
   himself hitting the ball.

3. What do you think will happen next in the story? Why?
   Ravi will get a hit. He is calm now, and he has practiced
   his swing. His sister is a good coach.

School–Home Connection
Have the student write a paragraph that continues the story.

Name _____

Review:
Homographs
Lesson 30

▲ Read each sentence. Then write a second sentence, using a different meaning of the underlined homograph. **Possible responses are shown.**

1. John plays the bass guitar in a band.
   I went fishing and caught a bass in the river.
   _____

2. There is an empty desk at the end of the row.
   It is your turn to row the boat.
   _____

3. My father loves to listen to his old records.
   Dr. Davis records information about her patients.
   _____

4. There is a tear in my jacket.
   A tear rolled down the actor's face.
   _____

5. I object to having too much homework over the winter holiday.
   What is that object in the closet?
   _____

6. I do not want to subject you to such a sad event.
   My favorite subject is English.
   _____

School-Home Connection

Make a homograph glossary with the student, using the words above. Have the student write the underlined word and then the definitions for both meanings.

Index

COMPREHENSION

GRAMMAR

Practice Book
© Harcourt • Grade 3

267

Practice Book
© Harcourt • Grade 3

266

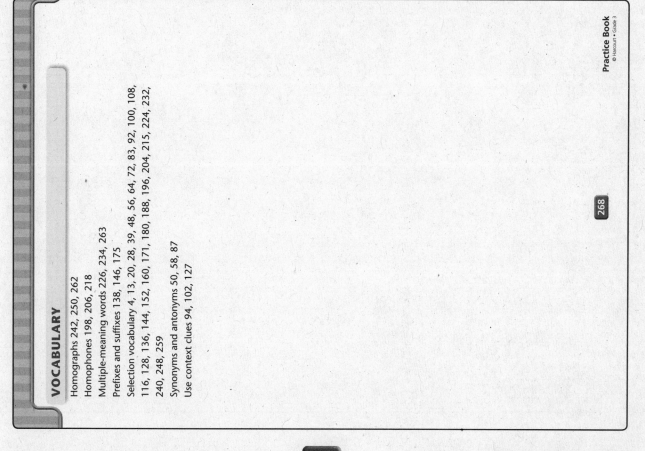

VOCABULARY

Homographs 242, 250, 262

Homophones 198, 206, 218

Multiple-meaning words 226, 234, 263

Prefixes and suffixes 138, 146, 175

Selection vocabulary 4, 13, 20, 28, 39, 48, 56, 64, 72, 83, 92, 100, 108, 116, 128, 136, 144, 152, 160, 171, 180, 188, 196, 204, 215, 224, 232, 240, 248, 259

Synonyms and antonyms 50, 58, 87

Use context clues 94, 102, 127